# THE MAN-EATERS OF TSAVO

John Henry Patterson

Printed and manufactured in the United States of America

# PREFACE

It is with feelings of the greatest diffidence that I place the following pages before the public; but those of my friends who happen to have heard of my rather unique experiences in the wilds have so often urged me to write an account of my adventures, that after much hesitation I at last determined to do so.

I have no doubt that many of my readers, who have perhaps never been very far away from civilisation, will be inclined to think that some of the incidents are exaggerated. I can only assure them that I have toned down the facts rather than otherwise, and have endeavoured to write a perfectly plain and straightforward account of things as they actually happened.

It must be remembered that at the time these events occurred, the conditions prevailing in British East Africa were very different from what they are to-day. The railway, which has modernised the aspect of the place and brought civilisation in its train, was then only in process of construction, and the country through which it was being built was still in its primitive savage state, as indeed, away from the railway, it still is.

If this simple account of two years' work and play in the wilds should prove of any interest, or help even in a small way to call attention to the beautiful and valuable country which we possess on the Equator, I shall feel more than compensated for the trouble I have taken in writing it.

I am much indebted to the Hon. Mrs. Cyril Ward, Sir Guilford Molesworth, K.C.I.E., Mr. T.J. Spooner and Mr C. Rawson for their kindness in allowing me to reproduce photographs taken by them. My warmest thanks are also due to that veteran pioneer of Africa, Mr. F.C. Selous, for giving my little book so kindly an introduction to the public as is provided by the "Foreword" which he has been good enough to write.

J.H.P.

3

# FOREWORD

It was some seven or eight years ago that I first read, in the pages of The Field newspaper, a brief account written by Col. J.H. Patterson, then an engineer engaged on the construction of the Uganda Railway, of the Tsavo man-eating lions.

My own long experience of African hunting told me at once that every word in this thrilling narrative was absolutely true. Nay more: I knew that the author had told his story in a most modest manner, laying but little stress on the dangers he had run when sitting up at nights to try and compass the death of the terrible man-eaters, especially on that one occasion when whilst watching from a very light scaffolding, supported only by four rickety poles, he was himself stalked by one of the dread beasts. Fortunately he did not lose his nerve, and succeeded in shooting the lion, just when it was on the point of springing upon him. But had this lion approached him from behind, I think it would probably have added Col. Patterson to its long list of victims, for in my own experience I have known of three instances of men having been pulled from trees or huts built on platforms at a greater height from the ground than the crazy structure on which Col. Patterson was watching on that night of terrors.

From the time of Herodotus until to-day, lion stories innumerable have been told and written. I have put some on record myself. But no lion story I have ever heard or read equals in its long-sustained and dramatic interest the story of the Tsavo man-eaters as told by Col. Patterson. A lion story is usually a tale of adventures, often very terrible and pathetic, which occupied but a few hours of one night; but the tale of the Tsavo man-eaters is an epic of terrible tragedies spread out over several months, and only at last brought to an end by the resource and determination of one man.

It was some years after I read the first account published of the Tsavo man-eaters that I made the acquaintance of President Roosevelt. I told him all I remembered about it, and he was so deeply interested in the story -- as he is in all true stories of the nature and characteristics of wild animals -- that he begged me to send him the short printed account as published in The Field. This I did; and it was only in the last letter I received from him that, referring to this story, President Roosevelt wrote: "I think that the incident of the Uganda man-eating lions, described in those two articles you sent me, is the most remarkable account of which we have any record. It is a great pity that it should not be preserved in permanent form." Well, I am now glad to think that it will be

4

preserved in permanent form; and I venture to assure Col. Patterson that President Roosevelt will be amongst the most interested readers of his book.

It is probable that the chapters recounting the story of the Tsavo man-eating lions will be found more absorbing than the other portions of Col. Patterson's book; but I think that most of his readers will agree with me that the whole volume is full of interest and information. The account given by Col. Patterson of how he overcame all the difficulties which confronted him in building a strong and permanent railway bridge across the Tsavo river makes excellent reading; whilst the courage he displayed in attacking, single-handed, lions, rhinoceroses and other dangerous animals was surpassed by the pluck, tact and determination he showed in quelling the formidable mutiny which once broke out amongst his native Indian workers.

Finally, let me say that I have spent the best part of two nights reading the proof-sheets of Col. Patterson's book, and I can assure him that the time passed like magic. My interest was held from the first page to the last, for I felt that every word I read was true.

F. C. SELOUS
WORPLESDON, SURREY

# TABLE OF CONTENTS

# CHAPTER I

## MY ARRIVAL AT TSAVO

It was towards noon on March 1, 1898, that I first found myself entering the narrow and somewhat dangerous harbour of Mombasa, on the east coast of Africa. The town lies on an island of the same name, separated from the mainland only by a very narrow channel, which forms the harbour; and as our vessel steamed slowly in, close under the quaint old Portuguese fortress built over three hundred years ago, I was much struck with the strange beauty of the view which gradually opened out before me. Contrary to my anticipation, everything looked fresh and green, and an oriental glamour of enchantment seemed to hang over the island. The old town was bathed in brilliant sunshine and reflected itself lazily on the motionless sea; its flat roofs and dazzlingly white walls peeped out dreamily between waving palms and lofty cocoanuts, huge baobabs and spreading mango trees; and the darker background of well-wooded hills and slopes on the mainland formed a very effective setting to a beautiful and, to me, unexpected picture.

The harbour was plentifully sprinkled with Arab dhows, in some of which, I believe, even at the present day, a few slaves are occasionally smuggled off to Persia and Arabia. It has always been a matter of great wonder to me how the navigators of little vessels find their way from port to port, as they do, without the aid of either compass or sextant, and how they manage to weather the terrible storms that at certain seasons of the year suddenly visit eastern seas. I remember once coming across a dhow becalmed in the middle of the Indian Ocean, and its crew making signals of distress, our captain slowed down to investigate. There were four men on board, all nearly dead from thirst; they had been without drink of any kind for several days and had completely lost their bearings. After giving them some casks of water, we directed them to Muscat (the port they wished to make), and our vessel resumed its journey, leaving them still becalmed in the midst of that glassy sea. Whether they managed to reach their destination I never knew.

As our steamer made its way to its anchorage, the romantic surroundings of the harbour of Mombasa conjured up, visions of stirring adventures of the past, and recalled to my mind the many tales of reckless doings of pirates and slavers, which as a boy it had been my delight to read. I remembered that it was at this very place that in 1498 the great Vasco da Gama nearly lost his ship and life through the treachery of his Arab pilot, who plotted to wreck the vessel on the reef which bars more than half the entrance to the harbour. Luckily, this nefarious design was discovered in time, and the bold navigator promptly hanged the pilot, and would also have sacked the town but for the timely submission and apologies of the Sultan. In the principal street of Mombasa -- appropriately called Vasco da Gama Street -- there still stands a curiously shaped pillar which is said to have been erected by this great seaman in commemoration of his visit.

Scarcely had the anchor been dropped, when, as if by magic, our vessel was surrounded by a fleet of small boats and "dug-outs" manned by crowds of shouting and gesticulating natives. After a short fight between some rival Swahili boatmen for my baggage and person, I found myself being vigorously rowed to the foot of the landing steps by the bahareen (sailors) who had been successful in the encounter. Now, my object in coming out to East Africa at this time was to take up a position to which I had been appointed by the Foreign Office on the construction staff of the Uganda Railway. As soon as I landed, therefore, I enquired from one of the Customs officials where the headquarters of the railway were to be found, and was told that they were at a place called Kilindini, some three miles away, on the other side of the island. The best way to get there, I was further informed, was by gharri, which I found to be a small trolley, having two seats placed back to back under a little canopy and running on narrow rails which are laid through the principal street of the town. Accordingly, I secured one of these vehicles, which are pushed by two strapping Swahili boys, and was soon flying down the track, which once outside the town lay for the most part through dense groves of mango, baobab, banana and palm trees, with here and there brilliantly coloured creepers hanging in luxuriant festoons from the branches.

On arrival at Kilindini, I made my way to the railway Offices and was informed that I should be stationed inland and should receive further instructions in the course of a day or two. Meanwhile I pitched my tent under some shady palms near the gharri line, and busied myself in exploring the island and in procuring the stores and the outfit necessary for a lengthy sojourn up-country. The town of Mombasa itself naturally occupied most of my attention. It is supposed to have been founded about A.D. 1000, but the discovery of ancient Egyptian idols, and of coins of the early Persian and Chinese dynasties, goes to show that it must at different ages have been settled by people of the very earliest civilisations. Coming to more modern times, it was held on and off from 1505 to 1729 by the Portuguese, a permanent memorial of whose occupation remains in the shape of the grim old fortress, built about 1593 -- on the site, it is believed, of a still older stronghold. These enterprising sea-rovers piously named it "Jesus Fort," and an inscription recording this is still to be seen over the main entrance. The Portuguese occupation of Mombasa was, however, not without its vicissitudes. From March 15, 1696, for example, the town was besieged for thirty-three consecutive months by a large fleet of Arab dhows, which completely surrounded the island. In spite of plague, treachery and famine, the little garrison held out valiantly in Jesus Fort, to which they had been forced to retire, until December 12, 1698, when the Arabs made a last determined attack and captured the citadel, putting the remnant of the defenders, both men and women, to the sword. It is pathetic to read that only two days later a large

Portuguese fleet appeared off the harbour, bringing the long-looked-for reinforcements. After this the Portuguese made several attempts to reconquer Mombasa, but were unsuccessful until 1728, when the town was stormed and captured by General Sampayo. The Arabs, however, returned the next year in overwhelming numbers, and again drove the Portuguese out; and although the latter made one more attempt in 1769 to regain their supremacy, they did not succeed.

The Arabs, as represented by the Sultan of Zanzibar, remain in nominal possession of Mombasa to the present day; but in 1887 Seyid Bargash, the then Sultan of Zanzibar, gave for an annual rental a concession of his mainland territories to the British East Africa Association, which in 1888 was formed into the Imperial British East Africa Company. In 1895 the Foreign Office took over control of the Company's possessions, and a Protectorate was proclaimed; and ten years later the administration of the country was transferred to the Colonial Office.

The last serious fighting on the island took place so recently as 1895-6, when a Swahili chief named M'baruk bin Rashed, who had three times previously risen in rebellion against the Sultan of Zanzibar, attempted to defy the British and to throw off their yoke. He was defeated on several occasions, however, and was finally forced to flee southwards into German territory. Altogether, Mombasa has in the past well deserved its native name of Kisiwa M'vitaa, or " Isle of War"; but under the settled rule now obtaining, it is rapidly becoming a thriving and prosperous town, and as the port of entry for Uganda, it does a large forwarding trade with the interior and has several excellent stores where almost anything, from a needle to an anchor, may readily be obtained.

Kilindini is, as I have said, on the opposite side of the island, and as its name -- "the place of deep waters" -- implies, has a much finer harbour than that possessed by Mombasa. The channel between the island and the mainland is here capable of giving commodious and safe anchorage to the very largest vessels, and as the jetty is directly connected with the Uganda Railway, Kilindini has now really become the principal port, being always used by the liners and heavier vessels.

I had spent nearly a week in Mombasa, and was becoming very anxious to get my marching orders, when one morning I was delighted to receive an official letter instructing me to proceed to Tsavo, about one hundred and thirty-two miles from the coast, and to take charge of the construction of the section of the line at that place, which had just then been reached by railhead. I accordingly started at daylight next morning in a special train with Mr. Anderson, the Superintendent of Works, and Dr. McCulloch, the principal Medical Officer; and as the country was in every way new to me, I found the journey a most interesting one.

The island of Mombasa is separated from the mainland by the Strait of Macupa, and the railway crosses this by a bridge about three-quarters of a mile long, called the Salisbury Bridge, in honour of the great Minister for Foreign Affairs under whose direction the

Uganda Railway scheme was undertaken. For twenty miles after reaching the mainland, our train wound steadily upwards through beautifully wooded, park-like country, and on looking back out of the carriage windows we could every now and again obtain lovely views of Mombasa and Kilindini, while beyond these the Indian Ocean sparkled in the glorious sunshine as far as the eye could see. The summit of the Rabai Hills having been reached, we entered on the expanse of the Taru Desert, a wilderness covered with poor scrub and stunted trees, and carpeted in the dry season with a layer of fine red dust. This dust is of a most penetrating character, and finds its way into everything in the carriage as the train passes along. From here onward game is more or less plentiful, but the animals are very difficult to see owing to the thick undergrowth in which they hide themselves. We managed, however, to catch sight of a few from the carriage windows, and also noticed some of the natives, the Wa Nyika, or "children of the wilderness."

At Maungu, some eighty miles from the coast, we came to the end of this "desert," but almost the only difference to be noticed in the character of the country was that the colour of the dust had changed. As our train sped onwards through the level uplands we saw a fine ostrich striding along parallel with the line, as if having a race with us. Dr. McCulloch at once seized his rifle and by a lucky shot brought down the huge bird; the next and greater difficulty, however, was to secure the prize. For a time the engine-driver took no notice of our signals and shouts, but at last we succeeded in attracting his attention, and the train was shunted back to where the ostrich had fallen. We found it to be an exceptionally fine specimen, and had to exert all our strength to drag it on board the train.

Soon after this we reached Voi, about a hundred miles from the coast, and as this was the most important station on the line that we had yet come to, we made a short halt in order to inspect some construction work which was going on. On resuming our journey, we soon discovered that a pleasant change had occurred in the character of the landscape. From a place called N'dii, the railway runs for some miles through a beautifully wooded country, which looked all the more inviting after the deadly monotony of the wilderness through which we had just passed. To the south of us could be seen the N'dii range of mountains, the dwelling-place of the Wa Taita people, while on our right rose the rigid brow of the N'dungu Escarpment, which stretches away westwards for scores of miles. Here our journey was slow, as every now and again we stopped to inspect the permanent works in progress; but eventually, towards dusk, we arrived at our destination, Tsavo. I slept that night in a little palm hut which had been built by some previous traveller, and which was fortunately unoccupied for the time being. It was rather broken-down and dilapidated, not even possessing a door, and as I lay on my narrow camp bed I could see the stars twinkling through the roof. I little knew then what adventures awaited me in this neighbourhood; and if I had realised that at that very time two savage brutes were prowling round, seeking whom they might devour, I hardly think I should have slept so peacefully in my rickety shelter.

Next morning I was up betimes, eager to make acquaintance with my new surroundings. My first impression on coming out of my hut was that I was hemmed in on all sides by a dense growth of impenetrable jungle: and on scrambling to the top of a little hill close at hand, I found that the whole country as far as I could see was covered with low, stunted trees, thick undergrowth and "wait-a-bit" thorns. The only clearing, indeed, appeared to be where the narrow track for the railway had been cut. This interminable nyika, or wilderness of whitish and leafless dwarf trees, presented a ghastly and sun-stricken appearance; and here and there a ridge of dark-red heat-blistered rock jutted out above the jungle, and added by its rugged barrenness to the dreariness of the picture. Away to the north-east stretched the unbroken line of the N'dungu Escarpment, while far off to the south I could just catch a glimpse of the snow-capped top of towering Kilima N'jaro. The one redeeming feature of the neighbourhood was the river from which Tsavo takes its name. This is a swiftly-flowing stream, always cool and always running, the latter being an exceptional attribute in this part of East Africa; and the fringe of lofty green trees along its banks formed a welcome relief to the general monotony of the landscape.

When I had thus obtained a rough idea of the neighbourhood, I returned to my hut, and began in earnest to make preparations for my stay in this out-of-the-way place. The stores were unpacked, and my "boys" pitched my tent in a little clearing close to where I had slept the night before and not far from the main camp of the workmen. Railhead had at this time just reached the western side of the river, and some thousands of Indian coolies and other workmen were encamped there. As the line had to be pushed on with all speed, a diversion had been made and the river crossed by means of a temporary bridge. My principal work was to erect the permanent structure, and to complete all the other works for a distance of thirty miles on each side of Tsavo. I accordingly made a survey of what had to be done, and sent my requisition for labour, tools and material to the head-quarters at Kilindini. In a short time workmen and supplies came pouring in, and the noise of hammers and sledges, drilling and blasting echoed merrily through the district.

# CHAPTER II

## THE FIRST APPEARANCE OF THE MAN-EATERS

Unfortunately this happy state of affairs did not continue for long, and our work was soon interrupted in a rude and startling manner. Two most voracious and insatiable man-eating lions appeared upon the scene, and for over nine months waged an intermittent warfare against the railway and all those connected with it in the vicinity of Tsavo. This culminated in a perfect reign of terror in December, 1898, when they actually succeeded in bringing the railway works to a complete standstill for about three weeks. At first they were not always successful in their efforts to carry off a victim, but as time went on they stopped at nothing and indeed braved any danger in order to obtain their favourite food. Their methods then became so uncanny, and their man-stalking so well-timed and so certain of success, that the workmen firmly believed that they were not real animals at all, but devils in lions' shape. Many a time the coolies solemnly assured me that it was absolutely useless to attempt to shoot them. They were quite convinced that the angry spirits of two departed native chiefs had taken this form in order to protest against a railway being made through their country, and by stopping its progress to avenge the insult thus shown to them.

I had only been a few days at Tsavo when I first heard that these brutes had been seen in the neighbourhood. Shortly afterwards one or two coolies mysteriously disappeared, and I was told that they had been carried off by night from their tents and devoured by lions. At the time I did not credit this story, and was more inclined to believe that the unfortunate men had been the victims of foul play at the hands of some of their comrades. They were, as it happened, very good workmen, and had each saved a fair number of rupees, so I thought it quite likely that some scoundrels from the gangs had murdered them for the sake of their money. This suspicion, however, was very soon dispelled. About three weeks after my arrival, I was roused one morning about daybreak and told that one of my jemadars, a fine powerful Sikh named Ungan Singh, had been seized in his tent during the night, and dragged off and eaten.

Naturally I lost no time in making an examination of the place, and was soon convinced that the man had indeed been carried off by a lion, as its "pug" marks were plainly visible in the sand, while the furrows made by the heels of the victim showed the direction in which he had been dragged away. Moreover, the jemadar shared his tent with half a dozen other workmen, and one of his bedfellows had actually witnessed the occurrence. He graphically described how, at about midnight, the lion suddenly put its head in at the open tent door and seized Ungan Singh -- who happened to be nearest the opening -- by the throat. The unfortunate fellow cried out "Choro" ("Let go"), and threw his arms up round the lion's neck. The next moment he was gone, and his panic-stricken companions lay helpless, forced to listen to the terrible struggle which took place outside. Poor Ungan Singh must have died hard; but what chance had he? As a coolie gravely remarked, "Was he not fighting with a lion?"

On hearing this dreadful story I at once set out to try to track the animal, and was accompanied by Captain Haslem, who happened to be staying at Tsavo at the time, and who, poor fellow, himself met with a tragic fate very shortly afterwards. We found it an easy matter to follow the route taken by the lion, as he appeared to have stopped several times before beginning his meal. Pools of blood marked these halting-places, where he doubtless indulged in the man-eaters' habit of licking the skin off so as to get at the fresh blood. (I have been led to believe that this is their custom from the appearance of two half-eaten bodies which I subsequently rescued: the skin was gone in places, and the flesh looked dry, as if it had been sucked.) On reaching the spot where the body had been devoured, a dreadful spectacle presented itself. The ground all round was covered with blood and morsels of flesh and bones, but the unfortunate jemadar's head had been left intact, save for the holes made by the lion's tusks on seizing him, and lay a short distance away from the other remains, the eyes staring wide open with a startled, horrified look in them. The place was considerably cut up, and on closer examination we found that two lions had been there and had probably struggled for possession of the body. It was the most gruesome sight I had ever seen. We collected the remains as well as we could and heaped stones on them, the head with its fixed, terrified stare seeming to watch us all the time, for it we did not bury, but took back to camp for identification before the Medical Officer.

Thus occurred my first experience of man-eating lions, and I vowed there and then that I would spare no pains to rid the neighbourhood of the brutes. I little knew the trouble that was in store for me, or how narrow were to be my own escapes from sharing poor Ungan Singh's fate.

That same night I sat up in a tree close to the late jemadar's tent, hoping that the lions would return to it for another victim. I was followed to my perch by a few of the more terrified coolies, who begged to be allowed to sit up in the tree with me; all the other workmen remained in their tents, but no more doors were left open. I had with me my . 303 and a 12-bore shot gun, one barrel loaded with ball and the other with slug. Shortly after settling down to my vigil, my hopes of bagging one of the brutes were raised by the sound of their ominous roaring coming closer and closer. Presently this ceased, and quiet reigned for an hour or two, as lions always stalk their prey in complete silence. All at once, however, we heard a great uproar and frenzied cries coming from another camp about half a mile away; we knew then that the lions had seized a victim there, and that we should see or hear nothing further of them that night.

Next morning I found that one of the brutes had broken into a tent at Railhead Camp -- whence we had heard the commotion during the night -- and had made off with a poor wretch who was lying there asleep. After a night's rest, therefore, I took up my position in a suitable tree near this tent. I did not at all like the idea of walking the half-mile to the place after dark, but all the same I felt fairly safe, as one of my men carried a bright lamp close behind me. He in his turn was followed by another leading a goat, which I tied under my tree in the hope that the lion might be tempted to seize it instead of a coolie. A steady drizzle commenced shortly after I had settled down to my night of watching, and I was soon thoroughly chilled and wet. I stuck to my uncomfortable post, however, hoping to get a shot, but I well remember the feeling of impotent disappointment I experienced when about midnight I heard screams and cries and a heart-rending shriek, which told me that the man-eaters had again eluded me and had claimed another victim elsewhere.

At this time the various camps for the workmen were very scattered, so that the lions had a range of some eight miles on either side of Tsavo to work upon; and as their tactics seemed to be to break into a different camp each night, it was most difficult to forestall them. They almost appeared, too, to have an extraordinary and uncanny faculty

14

of finding out our plans beforehand, so that no matter in how likely or how tempting a spot we lay in wait for them, they invariably avoided that particular place and seized their victim for the night from some other camp. Hunting them by day, moreover, in such a dense wilderness as surrounded us, was an exceedingly tiring and really foolhardy undertaking. In a thick jungle of the kind round Tsavo the hunted animal has every chance against the hunter, as however careful the latter may be, a dead twig or something of the sort is sure to crackle just at the critical moment and so give the alarm. Still I never gave up hope of some day finding their lair, and accordingly continued to devote all my spare time to crawling about through the undergrowth. Many a time when attempting to force my way through this bewildering tangle I had to be released by my gun-bearer from the fast clutches of the "wait-a-bit"; and often with immense pains I succeeded in tracing the lions to the river after they had seized a victim, only to lose the trail from there onwards, owing to the rocky nature of the ground which they seemed to be careful to choose in retreating to their den.

At this early stage of the struggle, I am glad to say, the lions were not always successful in their efforts to capture a human being for their nightly meal, and one or two amusing incidents occurred to relieve the tension from which our nerves were beginning to suffer. On one occasion an enterprising bunniah (Indian trader) was riding along on his donkey late one night, when suddenly a lion sprang out on him knocking over both man and beast. The donkey was badly wounded, and the lion was just about to seize the trader, when in some way or other his claws became entangled in a rope by which two empty oil tins were strung across the donkey's neck. The rattle and clatter made by these as he dragged them after him gave him such a fright that he turned tail and bolted off into the jungle, to the intense relief of the terrified bunniah, who quickly made his way up the nearest tree and remained there, shivering with fear, for the rest of the night.

Shortly after this episode, a Greek contractor named Themistocles Pappadimitrini had an equally marvellous escape. He was sleeping peacefully in his tent one night, when a lion broke in, and seized and made off with the mattress on which he was lying. Though, rudely awakened, the Greek was quite unhurt and suffered from nothing worse than a bad fright. This same man, however, met with a melancholy fate not long afterwards. He had been to the Kilima N'jaro district to buy cattle, and on the return journey attempted to take a short cut across country to the railway, but perished miserably of thirst on the way.

On another occasion fourteen coolies who slept together in a large tent were one night awakened by a lion suddenly jumping on to the tent and breaking through it. The brute landed with one claw on a coolie's shoulder, which was badly torn; but instead of seizing the man himself, in his hurry he grabbed a large bag of rice which happened to be lying in the tent, and made off with it, dropping it in disgust some little distance away when he realised his mistake.

These, however, were only the earlier efforts of the man-eaters. Later on, as will be seen, nothing flurried or frightened them in the least, and except as food they showed a complete contempt for human beings. Having once marked down a victim, they would allow nothing to deter them from securing him, whether he were protected by a thick fence, or inside a closed tent, or sitting round a brightly burning fire. Shots, shouting and firebrands they alike held in derision.

## CHAPTER III

### THE ATTACK ON THE GOODS-WAGON

All this time my own tent was pitched in an open clearing, unprotected by a fence of any kind round it. One night when the medical officer; Dr. Rose, was staying with me, we were awakened about midnight by hearing something tumbling about among the tent ropes, but on going out with a lantern we could discover nothing. Daylight, however, plainly revealed the "pug" marks of a lion, so that on that occasion I fancy one or other of us had a narrow escape. Warned by this experience, I at once arranged to move my quarters, and went to join forces with Dr. Brock, who had just arrived at Tsavo to take medical charge of the district. We shared a hut of palm leaves and boughs, which we had constructed on the eastern side of the river, close to the old caravan route leading to Uganda; and we had it surrounded by a circular boma, or thorn fence, about seventy yards in diameter, well made and thick and high. Our personal servants also lived within the enclosure, and a bright fire was always kept up throughout the night. For the sake of coolness, Brock and I used to sit out under the verandah of this hut in the evenings; but it was rather trying to our nerves to attempt to read or write there, as we never knew when a lion might spring over the boma, and be on us before we were aware. We therefore kept our rifles within easy reach, and cast many an anxious glance out into the inky darkness beyond the circle of the firelight. On one or two occasions, we found in the morning that the lions had come quite close to the fence; but fortunately they never succeeded in getting through.

By this time, too, the camps of the workmen had also been surrounded by thorn fences; nevertheless the lions managed to jump over or to break through some one or other of these, and regularly every few nights a man was carried off, the reports of the disappearance of this or that workman coming in to me with painful frequency. So long, however, as Railhead Camp -- with its two or three thousand men, scattered over a wide area -- remained at Tsavo, the coolies appeared not to take much notice of the dreadful deaths of their comrades. Each man felt, I suppose, that as the man-eaters had such a large number of victims to choose from, the chances of their selecting him in particular were very small. But when the large camp moved ahead with the railway, matters

16

altered considerably. I was then left with only some few hundred men to complete the permanent works; and as all the remaining workmen were naturally camped together, the attentions of the lions became more apparent and made a deeper impression. A regular panic consequently ensued, and it required all my powers of persuasion to induce the men to stay on. In fact, I succeeded in doing so only by allowing them to knock off all regular work until they had built exceptionally thick and high bomas round each camp. Within these enclosures fires were kept burning all night, and it was also the duty of the night-watchman to keep clattering half a dozen empty oil tins suspended from a convenient tree. These he manipulated by means of a long rope, while sitting in safety within his tent; and the frightful noise thus produced was kept up at frequent intervals during the night in the hopes of terrifying away the man-eaters. In spite of all these precautions, however, the lions would not be denied, and men continued to disappear.

When the railhead workmen moved on, their hospital camp was left behind. It stood rather apart from the other camps, in a clearing about three-quarters of a mile from my hut, but was protected by a good thick fence and to all appearance was quite secure. It seemed, however, as if barriers were of no avail against the "demons", for before very long one of them found a weak spot in the boma and broke through. On this occasion the Hospital Assistant had a marvellous escape. Hearing a noise outside, he opened the door of his tent and was horrified to see a great lion standing a few yards away looking at him. The beast made a spring towards him, which gave the Assistant such a fright that he jumped backwards, and in doing so luckily upset a box containing medical stores. This crashed down with such a loud clatter of breaking glass that the lion was startled for the moment and made off to another part of the enclosure. Here, unfortunately, he was more successful, as he jumped on to and broke through a tent in which eight patients were lying. Two of them were badly wounded by his spring, while a third poor wretch was seized and dragged off bodily through the thorn fence. The two wounded coolies were left where they lay, a piece of torn tent having fallen over them; and in this position the doctor and I found them on our arrival soon after dawn next morning. We at once decided to move the hospital closer to the main camp; a fresh site was prepared, a stout hedge built round the enclosure, and all the patients were moved in before nightfall.

As I had heard that lions generally visit recently deserted camps, I decided to sit up all night in the vacated boma in the hope of getting an opportunity of bagging one of them; but in the middle of my lonely vigil I had the mortification of hearing shrieks and cries coming from the direction of the new hospital, telling me only too plainly that our dreaded foes had once more eluded me. Hurrying to the place at daylight I found that one of the lions had jumped over the newly erected fence and had carried off the hospital bhisti (water-carrier), and that several other coolies had been unwilling witnesses of the terrible scene which took place within the circle of light given by the big camp fire. The bhisti, it appears, had been lying on the floor, with his head towards the centre of the tent and his feet neatly touching the side. The lion managed to get its head in below the canvas, seized him by the foot and pulled him out. In desperation the unfortunate water-carrier clutched hold of a heavy box in a vain attempt to prevent himself being carried off, and dragged it with him until he was forced to let go by its being stopped by the side of the tent. He then caught hold of a tent rope, and clung tightly to it until it broke. As soon as the lion managed to get him clear of the tent, he sprang at his throat and after a few vicious shakes the poor bhisti's agonising cries were silenced for ever. The brute then seized him in his mouth, like a huge cat with a mouse, and ran up and down the boma looking for a weak spot to break through. This he presently found and plunged into, dragging his victim with him and leaving shreds of torn cloth and flesh as ghastly evidences of his passage through the thorns. Dr. Brock and I were easily able to follow his track, and soon found the remains about four hundred yards away in the bush. There was the usual horrible sight. Very little was left of the unfortunate bhisti -- only the skull, the jaws, a few of the larger bones and a portion of the palm with one or two fingers attached. On one of these was a silver ring, and this, with the teeth (a relic much prized by certain castes), was sent to the man's widow in India.

Again it was decided to move the hospital; and again, before nightfall, the work was completed, including a still stronger and thicker boma. When the patients had been moved, I had a covered goods-wagon placed in a favourable position on a siding which ran close to the site which had just been abandoned, and in this Brock and I arranged to sit up that night. We left a couple of tents still standing within the enclosure, and also tied up a few cattle in it as bait for the lions, who had been seen in no less than three different places in the neighbourhood during the afternoon (April 23). Four miles from Tsavo they had attempted to seize a coolie who was walking along the line. Fortunately, however, he had just time to escape up a tree, where he remained, more dead than alive, until he was rescued by the Traffic Manager, who caught sight of him from a passing train. They next appeared close to Tsavo Station, and a couple of hours later some workmen saw one of the lions stalking Dr. Brock as he was returning about dusk from the hospital.

In accordance with our plan, the doctor and I set out after dinner for the goods-wagon, which was about a mile away from our hut. In the light of subsequent events, we did a very foolish thing in taking up our position so late; nevertheless, we reached our destination in safety, and settled down to our watch about ten o'clock. We had the lower half of the door of the wagon closed, while the upper half was left wide open for observation: and we faced, of course, in the direction of the abandoned boma, which, however, we were unable to see in the inky darkness. For an hour or two everything was quiet, and the deadly silence was becoming very monotonous and oppressive, when suddenly, to our right, a dry twig snapped, and we knew that an animal of some sort was about. Soon afterwards we heard a dull thud, as if some heavy body had jumped over the boma. The cattle, too, became very uneasy, and we could hear them moving about restlessly. Then again came dead silence. At this juncture I proposed to my companion that I should get out of the wagon and lie on the ground close to it, as I could see better in that position should the lion come in our direction with his prey. Brock, however, persuaded me to remain where I was; and a few seconds afterwards I was heartily glad that I had taken his advice, for at that very moment one of the man-eaters -- although we did not know it -- was quietly stalking us, and was even then almost within springing distance. Orders had been given for the entrance to the boma to be blocked up, and accordingly we were listening in the expectation of hearing the lion force his

18

way out through the bushes with his prey. As a matter of fact, however, the doorway had not been properly closed, and while we were wondering what the lion could be doing inside the boma for so long, he was outside all the time, silently reconnoitring our position.

Presently I fancied I saw something coming very stealthily towards us. I feared, however, to trust to my eyes, which by that time were strained by prolonged staring through the darkness, so under my breath I asked Brock whether he saw anything, at the same time covering the dark object as well as I could with my rifle. Brock did not answer; he told me afterwards that he, too, thought he had seen something move, but was afraid to say so lest I should fire and it turn out to be nothing after all. After this there was intense silence again for a second or two, then with a sudden bound a huge body sprang at us. "The lion!" I shouted, and we both fired almost simultaneously -- not a moment too soon, for in another second the brute would assuredly have landed inside the wagon. As it was, he must have swerved off in his spring, probably blinded by the flash and frightened by the noise of the double report which was increased a hundredfold by the reverberation of the hollow iron roof of the truck. Had we not been very much on the alert, he would undoubtedly have got one of us, and we realised that we had had a very lucky and very narrow escape. The next morning we found Brock's bullet embedded in the sand close to a footprint; it could not have missed the lion by more than an inch or two. Mine was nowhere to be found.

Thus ended my first direct encounter with one of the man-eaters.

## CHAPTER IV

### THE BUILDING OF THE TSAVO BRIDGE

During all this troublesome period the construction of the railway had been going steadily forward, and the first important piece of work which I had commenced on arrival was completed. This was the widening of a rock cutting through which the railway ran just before it, reached the river. In the hurry of pushing on the laying of the line, just enough of the rock had originally been cut away to allow room for an engine to pass, and consequently any material which happened to, project outside the wagons or trucks caught on the jagged faces of the cutting. I myself saw the door of a guard's van, which had been left ajar, smashed to atoms in this way; and accordingly I put a gang of rock-drillers to work at once and soon had ample room made for all traffic to pass unimpeded. While this was going on, another gang of men were laying the foundations of a girder bridge which was to span a gully between this cutting and Tsavo Station. This would have taken too long to erect when railhead was at the place, so a diversion had been made round it, the temporary track leading down almost to the bed of the nullah and up again on the further side. When the foundations and abutments were ready, the gully was spanned by an iron girder, the slopes leading up to it banked up on either side, and the permanent way laid on an easy grade.

Then, also, a water supply had to be established; and this meant some very pleasant work for me in taking levels up the banks of the river under the cool shade of the palms. While doing this, I often took my camp-kit with me, and a luncheon served in the wilds, with occasionally a friend to share it -- when a friend was available -- was delightful. On one occasion in particular, I went a long way up the river and was accompanied by a young member of my staff. The day had been exceedingly hot and we were both correspondingly tired when our work was finished, so my companion suggested that we should build a raft and float down-stream home. I was rather doubtful, of the feasibility of the scheme, but nevertheless he decided to give it a trial. Setting to work with our axes, we soon had a raft built, lashing the poles together with the fibre which grows in abundance all over the district. When it was finished, we pushed it out of the little backwater where it had been constructed, and the young engineer jumped aboard. All went well until it got out into midstream, when much to my amusement it promptly toppled gracefully over. I helped my friend to scramble quickly up the bank out of reach of possible crocodiles, when, none the worse for his ducking, he laughed as heartily as I at the adventure.

Except for an occasional relaxation of this sort, every moment of my time was fully occupied. Superintending the various works and a hundred other duties kept me busy all day long, while my evenings were given up to settling disputes among the coolies, hearing reports and complaints from the various jemadars and workpeople, and in studying the Swahili language. Preparations, too, for the principal piece of work in the district -- the building of the railway bridge over the Tsavo river -- were going on apace. These involved, much personal work on my part; cross and oblique sections of the river had to be taken, the rate of the current and the volume of water at flood, mean, and low levels had to be found, and all the necessary calculations made. These having at length been completed, I marked out the positions for the abutments and piers, and the work of sinking their foundations was begun. The two centre piers in particular caused a great deal of trouble, as the river broke in several times, and had to be dammed up and pumped dry again before work could be resumed. Then we found we had to sink much deeper than we expected in order to reach a solid foundation indeed, the sinking went on and on, until I began to despair of finding one and was about to resort to pile-driving, when at last, to my relief, we struck solid rock on which the huge foundation-stones could be laid with perfect safety.

Another great difficulty with which we had to contend was the absence of suitable stone in the neighbourhood. It was not that there was none to be found, for the whole district abounds in rock, but that it was so intensely hard as to be almost impossible to work, and a bridge built of it would have been very costly. I spent many a weary day trudging through the thorny wilderness vainly searching for suitable material, and was beginning to think that we should be forced to use iron columns for the piers, when one day I stumbled quite by accident on the very thing. Brock and I were out "pot-hunting," and hearing some guinea-fowl cackling among the bushes, I made a circuit half round them so that Brock, on getting in his shot, should drive them over in my direction. I eventually got into position on the edge of a deep ravine and knelt on one knee, crouching down among the ferns. There I had scarcely time to load when over flew a bird, which I missed badly; and I did not have another chance, for Brock had got to work, and being a first-rate shot had quickly bagged a brace. Meanwhile I felt the ground very hard under my knee, and on examination found that the bank of the ravine was formed of stone, which extended for some distance, and which was exactly the kind of material for which I had long been fruitlessly searching. I was greatly delighted with my unexpected discovery, though at first I had grave misgivings about the distance to be traversed and the difficulty of transporting the stone across the intervening country. Indeed, I found in the end that the only way of getting the material to the place where it was wanted was by laying down a tram line right along the ravine, throwing a temporary bridge across the Tsavo, following the stream down and re-crossing it again close to the site of the permanent bridge. Accordingly, I set men to work at once to cut down the jungle and prepare a road on which to lay the double trolley line. One morning when they were thus engaged, a little paa -- a kind of very small antelope -- sprang out and found itself suddenly in the midst of a gang of coolies. Terrified and confused by the shouting of the men, it ran straight at Shere Shah, the jemadar, who promptly dropped a basket over it and held it fast. I happened to arrive just in time to save the graceful little animal's life, and took it home to my camp, where it very soon became a great pet. Indeed, it grew so tame that it would jump upon my table at meal times and eat from my hand.

When the road for the trolley line was cleared, the next piece of work was the building of the two temporary bridges over the river. These we made in the roughest fashion out of palm trees and logs felled at the crossing places, and had a flood come down they would, of course, have both been swept away; fortunately, however, this did not occur until the permanent work was completed. The whole of this feeding line was finished in a very short time, and trollies were soon plying backwards and forwards with loads of stone and sand, as we also discovered the latter in abundance and of good quality in the bed of the ravine. An amusing incident occurred one day when I was taking a photograph of an enormous block of stone which was being hauled across one of these temporary bridges. As the trolley with its heavy load required very careful manipulation, my head mason, Heera Singh, stood on the top of the stone to direct operations, while the overseer, Purshotam Hurjee, superintended the gangs of men who hauled the ropes at either end in order to steady it up and down the inclines. But we did not know that the stream had succeeded in washing away the foundations of one of the log supports; and as the weight of the trolley with the stone came on the undermined pier, the rails tilted up and over went the whole thing into the river, just as I snapped the picture. Heera Singh made a wild spring into the water to get clear of the falling stone, while Purshotam and the rest fled as if for their lives to the bank. It was altogether a

21

most comical sight, and an extraordinary chance that at the very moment of the accident I should be taking a photograph of the operation. Fortunately, no one was injured in the slightest, and the stone was recovered undamaged with but little trouble.

Not long after this occurrence my own labours were one day nearly brought to a sudden and unpleasant end. I was travelling along in an empty trolley which, pushed by two sturdy Pathans, was returning to the quarry for sand. Presently we came to the sharp incline which led to the log bridge over the river. Here it was the custom of the men, instead of running beside the trolley, to step on to it and to let its own momentum take it down the slope, moderating its speed when necessary by a brake in the shape of a pole, which one of them carried and by which the wheels could be locked. On this occasion, however, the pole was by some accident dropped overboard, and down the hill we flew without brake of any kind. Near the bridge there was a sharp curve in the line, where I was afraid the trolley would jump the rails; still, I thought it was better to stick to it than to risk leaping off. A moment afterwards I felt myself flying head first over the edge of the bridge, just missing by a hair's breadth a projecting beam; but luckily I landed on a sand bank at the side of the river, the heavy trolley falling clear of me with a dull thud close by. This accident, also, was happily unattended by injury to anyone.

# CHAPTER V

## TROUBLES WITH THE WORKMEN

It seemed fated that the building of the Tsavo Bridge should never be allowed to proceed in peace for any length of time. I have already described our troubles with the lions; and no sooner did the beasts of prey appear to have deserted us, for the time being at any rate, than other troubles, no less serious, arose with the workmen themselves. After I had discovered the stone for the bridge, I sent down to the coast for gangs of masons to work and dress it. The men who were sent me for this purpose were mostly Pathans and were supposed to be expert workmen; but I soon found that many of them had not the faintest notion of stone-cutting, and were simply ordinary coolies who had posed as masons in order to draw forty-five instead of twelve rupees a month. On discovering this fact, I immediately instituted a system of piecework, and drew up a scale of pay which would enable the genuine mason to earn his forty-five rupees a month -- and a little more if he felt inclined -- and would cut down the impostors to about their proper pay as coolies. Now, as is often the case in this world, the impostors were greatly in the majority; and accordingly they attempted to intimidate the remainder into coming down to their own standard as regards output of work, in the hope of thereby inducing me to abandon the piece-work system of payment. This, however, I had no intention of doing, as I knew that I had demanded only a perfectly fair amount of work from each man.

These masons were continually having quarrels and fights amongst themselves, and I had frequently to go down to their camp to quell disturbances and to separate the Hindus from the Mohammedans. One particularly serious disturbance of this sort had a rather amusing sequel. I was sitting after dusk one evening at the door of my hut, when I heard a great commotion in the masons' camp, which lay only a few hundred yards away. Presently a jemadar came rushing up to me to say that the men were all fighting and murdering each other with sticks and stones. I ran back with him at once and succeeded in restoring order, but found seven badly injured men lying stretched out on the ground. These I had carried up to my own boma on charpoys (native beds); and Brock being away, I had to play the doctor myself as best I could, stitching one and bandaging another and generally doing what was possible. There was one man, however, who groaned loudly and held a cloth over his face as if he were dying. On lifting this covering, I found him to be a certain mason called Karim Bux, who was well known to me as a prime mischief-maker among the men. I examined him carefully, but as I could discover nothing amiss, I concluded that he must have received some internal injury, and accordingly told him that I would send him to the hospital at Voi (about thirty miles down the line) to be attended to properly. He was then carried back to his camp, groaning grievously all the time.

Scarcely had he been removed, when the head jemadar came and informed me that the man was not hurt at all, and that as a matter of fact he was the sole cause of the disturbance. He was now pretending to be badly injured, in order to escape the punishment which he knew he would receive if I discovered that he was the instigator of the trouble. On hearing this, I gave instructions that he was not to go to Voi in the special train with the others; but I had not heard the last of him yet. About eleven o'clock that night I was called up and asked to go down to the masons' camp to see a man who was supposed to be dying. I at once pulled on my boots, got some brandy and ran down to the camp, where to my surprise and amusement I found that it was my friend Karim Bux who was at death's door. It was perfectly evident to me that he was only "foxing," but when he asked for dawa (medicine), I told him gravely that I would give him some very good dawa in the morning.

Next day at noon -- when it was my custom to have evil-doers brought up for judgment -- I asked for Karim Bux, but was told that he was too ill to walk. I accordingly ordered him to be carried to my boma, and in a few moments he arrived in his charpoy, which was shouldered by four coolies who, I could see, knew quite well that he was only shamming. There were also a score or so of his friends hanging around, doubtless waiting in the expectation of seeing the "Sahib" hoodwinked. When the bed was placed on the ground near me, I lifted the blanket with which he had covered himself and thoroughly examined him, at the same time feeling him to make sure that he had no fever. He pretended to be desperately ill and again asked for dawa; but having finally

23

satisfied myself that it was as the jemadar had said -- pure budmashi (devilment) -- I told him that I was going to give him some very effective dawa, and carefully covered him up again, pulling the blanket over his head. I then got a big armful of shavings from a carpenter's bench which was close by, put them under the bed and set fire to them. As soon as the sham invalid felt the heat, he peeped over the edge of the blanket; and when he saw the smoke and flame leaping up round him, he threw the blanket from him, sprang from the bed exclaiming "Beiman shaitan!" ("Unbelieving devil!"), and fled like a deer to the entrance of my boma, pursued by a Sikh sepoy, who got in a couple of good whacks on his shoulders with a stout stick before he effected his escape. His amused comrades greeted me with shouts of "Shabash, Sahib!" ("Well done, sir"), and I never had any further trouble with Karim Bux. He came back later in the day, with clasped hands imploring forgiveness, which I readily granted, as he was a clever workman.

A few days after this incident I was returning home one morning from a tree in which I had been keeping watch for the man-eaters during the previous night. Coming unexpectedly on the quarry, I was amazed to find dead silence reigning and my rascals of workmen all stretched out in the shade under the trees taking it very easy -- some sleeping, some playing cards. I watched their proceedings through the bushes for a little while, and then it occurred to me to give them a fright by firing my rifle over their heads. On the report being heard, the scene changed like magic: each man simply flew to his particular work, and hammers and chisels resounded merrily and energetically, where all had been silence a moment before. They thought, of course, that I was still some distance off and had not seen them, but to their consternation I shouted to them that they were too late, as I had been watching them for some time. I fined every man present heavily, besides summarily degrading the Headman, who had thus shown himself utterly unfit for his position. I then proceeded to my hut, but had scarcely arrived there when two of the scoundrels tottered up after me, bent almost double and calling Heaven to witness that I had shot them both in the back. In order to give a semblance of truth to an otherwise bald and unconvincing narrative, they had actually induced one of their fellow workmen to make a few holes like shot holes in their backs, and these were bleeding profusely. Unfortunately for them, however, I had been carrying a rifle and not a shot gun, and they had also forgotten to make corresponding holes in their clothing, so that all they achieved by this elaborate tissue of falsehood was to bring on themselves the derision of their comrades and the imposition of an extra fine.

Shortly after this, when the masons realised that I intended to make each man do a fair day's work for his money, and would allow nothing to prevent this intention from being carried out, they came to the conclusion that the best thing to do would be to put me quietly out of the way. Accordingly they held a meeting one night, all being sworn to secrecy, and after a long palaver it was arranged that I was to be murdered next day when I made my usual visit to the quarry. My body was to be thrown into the jungle, where of course it would soon be devoured by wild beasts, and then they were to say that I had been killed and eaten by a lion. To this cheerful proposal every man present at the meeting agreed, and affixed his finger-mark to a long strip of paper as a binding token. Within an hour after the meeting had dispersed, however, I was aroused by one

24

of the conspirators, who had crept into my camp to give me warning. I thanked him for his information, but determined to go to the quarry in the morning all the same, as at this stage of affairs I really did not believe that they were capable of carrying out such a diabolical scheme, and was rather inclined to think that the informant had been sent merely to frighten me.

Accordingly the next morning (September 6) I started off as usual along the trolley line to the lonely quarry. As I reached a bend in the line, my head mason, Heera Singh, a very good man, crept cautiously out of the bushes and warned me not to proceed. On my asking him the reason, he said that he dared not tell, but that he and twenty other masons were not going to work that day, as they were afraid of trouble at the quarry. At this I began to think that there was something in the story I had heard overnight, but I laughingly assured him there would be no trouble and continued on my way. On my arrival at the quarry, everything seemed perfectly peaceful. All the men were working away busily, but after a moment or two I noticed stealthy side glances, and felt that there was something in the wind. As soon as I came up to the first gang of workmen, the jemadar, a treacherous-looking villain, informed me that the men working further up the ravine had refused to obey his orders, and asked me if I would go and see them. I felt at once that this was a device to lure me into the narrow part of the ravine, where, with gangs in front of me and behind me, there would be no escape; still I thought I would see the adventure through, whatever came of it, so I accompanied the jemadar up the gully. When we got to the further gang, he went so far as to point out the two men who, he said, had refused to do what he told them -- I suppose he thought that as I was never to leave the place alive, it did not matter whom he complained of. I noted their names in my pocket-book in my usual manner, and turned to retrace my steps. Immediately a yell of rage was raised by the whole body of some sixty men, answered by a similar shout from those I had first passed, and who numbered about a hundred. Both groups of men, carrying crowbars and flourishing their heavy hammers, then closed in on me in the narrow part of the ravine. I stood still, waiting for them to act, and one man rushed at me, seizing both my wrists and shouting out that he was going to "be hung and shot for me" -- rather a curious way of putting it, but that was his exact expression. I easily wrenched my arms free, and threw him from me; but by this time I was closely hemmed in, and everywhere I looked I could see nothing but evil and murderous-looking faces. One burly brute, afraid to be the first to deal a blow, hurled the man next him at me; and if he had succeeded in knocking me down, I am certain that I should never have got up again alive. As it was, however, I stepped quickly aside, and the man intended to knock me down was himself thrown violently against a rock, over which he fell heavily.

This occasioned a moment's confusion, of which I quickly took advantage. I sprang on to the top of the rock, and before they had time to recover themselves I had started haranguing them in Hindustani. The habit of obedience still held them, and fortunately they listened to what I had to say. I told them that I knew all about their plot to murder me, and that they could certainly do so if they wished; but that if they did, many of them would assuredly be hanged for it, as the Sirkar (Government) would soon find out the truth and would disbelieve their story that I had been carried off by a lion. I said that I knew quite well that it was only one or two scoundrels among them who had induced them to behave so stupidly, and urged them not to allow themselves to be made fools of in this way. Even supposing they were to carry out their plan of killing me, would not another "Sahib "at once be set over them, and might he not be an even harder task-master? They all knew that I was just and fair to the real worker; it was only the scoundrels and shirkers who had anything to fear from me, and were upright, self-respecting. Pathans going to allow themselves to be led away by men of that kind? Once having got them to listen to me, I felt a little more secure, and I accordingly went on to say that the discontented among them would be allowed to return at once to Mombasa, while if the others resumed work and I heard of no further plotting, I would take no notice of their foolish conduct. Finally I called upon those who were willing to return to work to hold up their hands, and instantly every hand in the crowd was raised. I then felt that for the moment the victory was mine, and after dismissing them, I jumped down from the rock and continued my rounds as if nothing had happened, measuring a stone here and there and commenting on the work done. They were still in a very uncertain and sullen mood, however, and not at all to be relied upon, so it was with feelings of great relief that an hour later I made my way back, safe and sound, to Tsavo.

The danger was not yet past, unfortunately, for scarcely had I turned my back to go home when the mutiny broke out again, another meeting being held, and a fresh plot made to murder me during the night. Of this I was soon informed by my time-keeper, who also told me that he was afraid to go out and call the roll, as they had threatened to kill him also. At this further outrage I lost no time in telegraphing for the Railway Police, and also to the District Officer, Mr. Whitehead, who immediately marched his men twenty-five miles by road to my assistance. I have no doubt, indeed, that his prompt action alone saved me from being attacked that very night. Two or three days afterwards the Railway Police arrived and arrested the ringleaders in the mutiny, who were taken to Mombasa and tried before Mr. Crawford, the British Consul, when the full details of the plots to murder me were unfolded by one of them who turned Queen's evidence. All the scoundrels were found guilty and sentenced to various terms of imprisonment in the chain-gangs, and I was never again troubled with mutinous workmen.

# CHAPTER VI

## THE REIGN OF TERROR

The lions seemed to have got a bad fright the night Brock and I sat up in wait for them in the goods-wagon, for they kept away from Tsavo and did not molest us in any way for some considerable time -- not, in fact, until long after Brock had left me and gone on safari (a caravan journey) to Uganda. In this breathing space which they vouchsafed us, it occurred to me that should they renew their attacks, a trap would perhaps offer the best chance of getting at them, and that if I could construct one in which a couple of coolies might be used as bait without being subjected to any danger, the lions would be quite daring enough to enter it in search of them and thus be caught. I accordingly set to work at once, and in a short time managed to make a sufficiently strong trap out of wooden sleepers, tram-rails, pieces of telegraph wire, and a length of heavy chain. It was divided into two compartments -- one for the men and one for the lion. A sliding door at one end admitted the former, and once inside this compartment they were perfectly safe, as between them and the lion, if he entered the other, ran a cross wall of iron rails only three inches apart, and embedded both top and bottom in heavy wooden sleepers. The door which was to admit the lion was, of course, at the opposite end of the structure, but otherwise the whole thing was very much on the principle of the ordinary rat-trap, except that it was not necessary for the lion to seize the bait in order to send the door clattering down. This part of the contrivance was arranged in the following manner. A heavy chain was secured along the top part of the lion's doorway, the ends hanging down to the ground on either side of the opening; and to these were fastened, strongly secured by stout wire, short lengths of rails placed about six inches apart. This made a sort of flexible door which could be packed into a small space when not in use, and which abutted against the top of the doorway when lifted up. The door was held in this position by a lever made of a piece of rail, which in turn was kept in its place by a wire fastened to one end and passing down to a spring concealed in the ground inside the cage. As soon as the lion entered sufficiently far into the trap, he would be bound to tread on the spring; his weight on this would release the wire, and in an instant down would come the door behind him; and he could not push it out in any way, as it fell into a groove between two rails firmly embedded in the ground.

In making this trap, which cost us a lot of work, we were rather at a loss for want of tools to bore holes in the rails for the doorway, so as to enable them to be fastened by the wire to the chain. It occurred to me, however, that a hard-nosed bullet from my .303 would penetrate the iron, and on making the experiment I was glad to find that a hole was made as cleanly as if it had been punched out.

When the trap was ready I pitched a tent over it in order further to deceive the lions, and built an exceedingly strong boma round it. One small entrance was made at the back of the enclosure for the men, which they were to close on going in by pulling a bush after them; and another entrance just in front of the door of the cage was left open for the

27

lions. The wiseacres to whom I showed my invention were generally of the opinion that the man-eaters would be too cunning to walk into my parlour; but, as will be seen later, their predictions proved false. For the first few nights I baited the trap myself, but nothing happened except that I had a very sleepless and uncomfortable time, and was badly bitten by mosquitoes.

As a matter of fact, it was some months before the lions attacked us again, though from time to time we heard of their depredations in other quarters. Not long after our night in the goods-wagon, two men were carried off from railhead, while another was taken from a place called Engomani, about ten miles away. Within a very short time, this latter place was again visited by the brutes, two more men being seized, one of whom was killed and eaten, and the other so badly mauled that he died within few days. As I have said, however, we at Tsavo enjoyed complete immunity from attack, and the coolies, believing that their dreaded foes had permanently deserted the district, resumed all their usual habits and occupations, and life in the camps returned to its normal routine.

At last we were suddenly startled out of this feeling of security. One dark night the familiar terror-stricken cries and screams awoke the camps, and we knew that the "demons" had returned and had commenced a new list of victims. On this occasion a number of men had been sleeping outside their tents for the sake of coolness, thinking, of course, that the lions had gone for good, when suddenly in the middle of the night one of the brutes was discovered forcing its way through the boma. The alarm was at once given, and sticks, stones and firebrands were hurled in the direction of the intruder. All was of no avail, however, for the lion burst into the midst of the terrified group, seized an unfortunate wretch amid the cries and shrieks of his companions, and dragged him off through the thick thorn fence. He was joined outside by the second lion, and so daring had the two brutes become that they did not trouble to carry their victim any further away, but devoured him within thirty yards of the tent where he had been seized. Although several shots were fired in their direction by the jemadar of the gang to which the coolie belonged, they took no notice of these and did not attempt to move until their horrible meal was finished. The few scattered fragments that remained of the body I would not allow to be buried at once, hoping that the lions would return to the spot the following night; and on the chance of this I took up my station at nightfall in a convenient tree. Nothing occurred to break the monotony of my watch, however, except that I had a visit from a hyena, and the next morning I learned that the lions had attacked another camp about two miles from Tsavo -- for by this time the camps were again scattered, as I had works in progress all up and down the line. There the man-eaters had been successful in obtaining a victim, whom, as in the previous instance, they devoured quite close to the camp. How they forced their way through the bomas without making a noise was, and still is, a mystery to me; I should have thought that it was next to impossible for an animal to get through at all. Yet they continually did so, and without a sound being heard.

After this occurrence, I sat up every night for over a week near likely camps, but all in vain. Either the lions saw me and then went elsewhere, or else I was unlucky, for they took man after man from different places without ever once giving me a chance of a shot at them. This constant night watching was most dreary and fatiguing work, but I felt that it was a duty that had to be undertaken, as the men naturally looked to me for protection. In the whole of my life I have never experienced anything more nerve-shaking than to hear the deep roars of these dreadful monsters growing gradually nearer and nearer, and to know that some one or other of us was doomed to be their victim before morning dawned. Once they reached the vicinity of the camps, the roars completely ceased, and we knew that they were stalking for their prey. Shouts would then pass from camp to camp, "Khabar dar, bhaieon, shaitan ata" (" Beware, brothers, the devil is coming "), but the warning cries would prove of no avail, and sooner or later agonising shrieks would break the silence, and another man would be missing from roll-call next morning.

I was naturally very disheartened at being foiled in this way night after night, and was soon at my wits' end to know what to do; it seemed as if the lions were really "devils" after all and bore a charmed life. As I have said before, tracking them through the jungle was a hopeless task; but as something had to be done to keep up the men's spirits, I spent many a weary day crawling on my hands and knees through the dense undergrowth of the exasperating wilderness around us. As a matter of fact, if I had come up with the lions on any of these expeditions, it was much more likely that they would have added me to their list of victims than that I should have succeeded in killing either of them, as everything would have been in their favour. About this time, too, I had many helpers, and several officers -- civil, naval and military -- came to Tsavo from the coast and sat up night after night in order to get a shot at our daring foes. All of us, however, met with the same lack of success, and the lions always seemed capable of avoiding the watchers, while succeeding, at the same time in obtaining a victim.

I have a very vivid recollection of one particular night when the brutes seized a man from the railway station and brought him close to my camp to devour. I could plainly hear them crunching the bones, and the sound of their dreadful purring filled the air and rang in my ears for days afterwards. The terrible thing was to feel so helpless; it was useless to attempt to go out, as of course the poor fellow was dead, and in addition it was so pitch dark as to make it impossible to see anything. Some half a dozen workmen, who lived in a small enclosure close to mine, became so terrified on hearing the lions at their meal that they shouted and implored me to allow them to come inside my boma. This I willingly did, but soon afterwards I remembered that one man had been lying ill in their camp, and on making enquiry I found that they had callously left him behind alone. I immediately took some men with me to bring him to my boma, but on entering his tent I saw by the light of the lantern that the poor fellow was beyond need of safety. He had died of shock at being deserted by his companions.

From this time matters gradually became worse and worse. Hitherto, as a rule, only one of the man-eaters had made the attack and had done the foraging, while the other waited outside in the bush; but now they began to change their tactics, entering the bomas together and each seizing a victim. In this way two Swahili porters were killed during the last week of November, one being immediately carried off and devoured. The other was heard moaning for a long time, and when his terrified companions at last summoned up sufficient courage to go to his assistance, they found him stuck fast in the bushes of the boma, through which for once the lion had apparently been unable to drag him. He was still alive when I saw him next morning, but so terribly mauled that he died before he could be got to the hospital.

Within a few days of this the two brutes made a most ferocious attack on the largest camp in the section, which for safety's sake was situated within a stone's throw of Tsavo Station and close to a Permanent Way Inspector's iron hut. Suddenly in the dead of night the two man-eaters burst in among the terrified workmen, and even from my boma, some distance away, I could plainly hear the panic-stricken shrieking of the coolies. Then followed cries of "They've taken him; they've taken him," as the brutes carried off their unfortunate victim and began their horrible feast close beside the camp. The Inspector, Mr. Dalgairns, fired over fifty shots in the direction in which he heard the lions, but they were not to be frightened and calmly lay there until their meal was finished. After examining the spot in the morning, we at once set out to follow the brutes, Mr. Dalgairns feeling confident that he had wounded one of them, as there was a trail on the sand like that of the toes of a broken limb. After some careful stalking, we suddenly found ourselves in the vicinity of the lions, and were greeted with ominous growlings. Cautiously advancing and pushing the bushes aside, we saw in the gloom what we at first took to be a lion cub; closer inspection, however, showed it to be the remains of the unfortunate coolie, which the man-eaters had evidently abandoned at our approach. The legs, one arm and half the body had been eaten, and it was the stiff fingers of the other arm trailing along the sand which had left the marks we had taken to be the trail of a wounded lion. By this time the beasts had retired far into the thick jungle where it was impossible to follow them, so we had the remains of the coolie buried and once more returned home disappointed.

Now the bravest men in the world, much less the ordinary Indian coolie, will not stand constant terrors of this sort indefinitely. The whole district was by this time thoroughly panic-stricken, and I was not at all surprised, therefore, to find on my return to camp that same afternoon (December 1) that the men had all struck work and were waiting to speak to me. When I sent for them, they flocked to my boma in a body and stated that they would not remain at Tsavo any longer for anything or anybody; they had come from India on an agreement to work for the Government, not to supply food for either lions or "devils." No sooner had they delivered this ultimatum than a regular stampede took place. Some hundreds of them stopped the first passing train by throwing themselves on the rails in front of the engine, and then, swarming on to the trucks and throwing in their possessions anyhow, they fled from the accursed spot.

After this the railway works were completely stopped; and for the next three weeks practically nothing was done but build "lion-proof" huts for those workmen who had had sufficient courage to remain. It was a strange and amusing sight to see these shelters perched on the top of water-tanks, roofs and girders -- anywhere for safety -- while some even went so far as to dig pits inside their tents, into which they descended at night, covering the top over with heavy logs of wood. Every good-sized tree in the camp had as many beds lashed on to it as its branches would bear -- and sometimes more. I remember that one night when the camp was attacked, so many men swarmed on to one particular tree that down it came with a crash, hurling its terror-stricken load of shrieking coolies close to the very lions they were trying to avoid. Fortunately for them, a victim had already been secured, and the brutes were too busy devouring him to pay attention to anything else.

# CHAPTER VII

## THE DISTRICT OFFICER'S NARROW ESCAPE

Some little time before the flight of the workmen, I had written to Mr. Whitehead, the District Officer, asking him to come up and assist me in my campaign against the lions, and to bring with him any of his askaris (native soldiers) that he could spare. He replied accepting the invitation, and told me to expect him about dinner-time on December 2, which turned out to be the day after the exodus. His train was due at Tsavo about six o'clock in the evening, so I sent my "boy" up to the station to meet him and to help in carrying his baggage to the camp. In a very short time, however, the "boy" rushed back trembling with terror, and informed me that there was no sign of the train or of the railway staff, but that an enormous lion was standing on the station platform. This extraordinary story I did not believe in the least, as by this time the coolies -- never remarkable for bravery -- were in such a state of fright that if they caught sight of a hyena or a baboon, or even a dog, in the bush, they were sure to imagine it was a lion; but I found out next day that it was an actual fact, and that both stationmaster and signalman had been obliged to take refuge from one of the man-eaters by locking themselves in the station building.

I waited some little time for Mr. Whitehead, but eventually, as he did not put in an appearance, I concluded that he must have postponed his journey until the next day, and so had my dinner in my customary solitary state. During the meal I heard a couple of shots, but paid no attention to them, as rifles were constantly being fired off in the neighbourhood of the camp. Later in the evening, I went out as usual to watch for our elusive foes, and took up my position in a crib made of sleepers which I had built on a big girder close to a camp which I thought was likely to be attacked. Soon after settling down at my post, I was surprised to hear the man-eaters growling and purring and crunching up bones about seventy yards from the crib. I could not understand what they had found to eat, as I had heard no commotion in the camps, and I knew by bitter experience that every meal the brutes obtained from us was announced by shrieks and uproar. The only conclusion I could come to was that they had pounced upon some poor unsuspecting native traveller. After a time I was able to make out their eyes glowing in the darkness, and I took as careful aim as was possible in the circumstances and fired; but the only notice they paid to the shot was to carry off whatever they were devouring and to retire quietly over a slight rise, which prevented me from seeing them. There they finished their meal at their ease.

As soon as it was daylight, I got out of my crib and went towards the place where I had last heard them. On the way, whom should I meet but my missing guest, Mr. Whitehead, looking very pale and ill, and generally dishevelled.

"Where on earth have you come from?" I exclaimed. "Why didn't you turn up to dinner last night?"

"A nice reception you give a fellow when you invite him to dinner," was his only reply.

"Why, what's up?" I asked.

"That infernal lion of yours nearly did for me last night," said Whitehead.

"Nonsense, you must have dreamed it!" I cried in astonishment.

For answer he turned round and showed me his back. "That's not much of a dream, is it?" he asked.

His clothing was rent by one huge tear from the nape of the neck downwards, and on the flesh there were four great claw marks, showing red and angry through the torn cloth. Without further parley, I hurried him off to my tent, and bathed and dressed his wounds; and when I had made him considerably more comfortable, I got from him the whole story of the events of the night.

It appeared that his train was very late, so that it was quite dark when he arrived at Tsavo Station, from which the track to my camp lay through a small cutting. He was accompanied by Abdullah, his sergeant of askaris, who walked close behind him carrying a lighted lamp. All went well until they were about half-way through the gloomy cutting, when one of the lions suddenly jumped down upon them from the high bank, knocking Whitehead over like a ninepin, and tearing his back in the manner I had seen. Fortunately, however, he had his carbine with him, and instantly fired. The flash and the loud report must have dazed the lion for a second or two, enabling Whitehead to disengage himself; but the next instant the brute pounced like lightning on the unfortunate Abdullah, with whom he at once made off. All that the poor fellow could say was: "Eh, Bwana, simba" (" Oh, Master, a lion "). As the lion was dragging him over the bank, Whitehead fired again, but without effect, and the brute quickly

32

disappeared into the darkness with his prey. It was of course, this unfortunate man whom I had heard the lions devouring during the night. Whitehead himself had a marvellous escape; his wounds were happily not very deep, and caused him little or no inconvenience afterwards.

On the same day, December 3, the forces arrayed against the lions were further strengthened. Mr. Farquhar, the Superintendent of Police, arrived from the coast with a score of sepoys to assist in hunting down the man-eaters, whose fame had by this time spread far and wide, and the most elaborate precautions were taken, his men being posted on the most convenient trees near every camp. Several other officials had also come up on leave to join in the chase, and each of these guarded a likely spot in the same way, Mr. Whitehead sharing my post inside the crib on the girder. Further, in spite of some chaff, my lion trap was put in thorough working order, and two of the sepoys were installed as bait.

Our preparations were quite complete by nightfall, and we all took up our appointed positions. Nothing happened until about nine o'clock, when to my great satisfaction the intense stillness was suddenly broken by the noise of the door of the trap clattering down. "At last," I thought, "one at least of the brutes is done for." But the sequel was an ignominious one.

The bait-sepoys had a lamp burning inside their part of the cage, and were each armed with a Martini rifle, with plenty of ammunition. They had also been given strict orders to shoot at once if a lion should enter the trap. Instead of doing so, however, they were so terrified when he rushed in and began to lash himself madly against the bars of the cage, that they completely lost their heads and were actually too unnerved to fire. Not for some minutes -- not, indeed, until Mr. Farquhar, whose post was close by, shouted at them and cheered them on -- did they at all recover themselves. Then when at last they did begin to fire, they fired with a vengeance -- anywhere, anyhow. Whitehead and I were at right angles to the direction in which they should have shot, and yet their bullets came whizzing all round us. Altogether they fired over a score of shots, and in the end succeeded only in blowing away one of the bars of the door, thus allowing our prize to make good his escape. How they failed to kill him several times over is, and always will be, a complete mystery to me, as they could have put the muzzles of their rifles absolutely touching his body. There was, indeed, some blood scattered about the trap, but it was small consolation to know that the brute, whose capture and death seemed so certain, had only been slightly wounded.

Still we were not unduly dejected, and when morning came, a hunt was at once arranged. Accordingly we spent the greater part of the day on our hands and knees following the lions through the dense thickets of thorny jungle, but though we heard their growls from time to time, we never succeeded in actually coming up with them. Of the whole party, only Farquhar managed to catch a momentary glimpse of one as it bounded over a bush. Two days more were spent in the same manner, and with equal unsuccess; and then Farquhar and his sepoys were obliged to return to the coast. Mr.

Whitehead also departed for his district, and once again I was left alone with the man-eaters.

## CHAPTER VIII

### THE DEATH OF THE FIRST MAN-EATER

A day or two after the departure of my allies, as I was leaving my boma soon after dawn on December 9, I saw a Swahili running excitedly towards me, shouting out "Simba! Simba!" ("Lion! Lion!"), and every now and again looking behind him as he ran. On questioning him I found that the lions had tried to snatch a man from the camp by the river, but being foiled in this had seized and killed one of the donkeys, and were at that moment busy devouring it not far off. Now was my chance.

I rushed for the heavy rifle which Farquhar had kindly left with me for use in case an opportunity such as this should arise, and, led by the Swahili, I started most carefully to stalk the lions, who, I devoutly hoped, were confining their attention strictly to their meal. I was getting on splendidly, and could just make out the outline of one of them through the dense bush, when unfortunately my guide snapped a rotten branch. The wily beast heard the noise, growled his defiance, and disappeared in a moment into a patch of even thicker jungle close by. In desperation at the thought of his escaping me once again, I crept hurriedly back to the camp, summoned the available workmen and told them to bring all the tom-toms, tin cans, and other noisy instruments of any kind that could be found. As quickly as possible I posted them in a half-circle round the thicket, and gave the head jemadar instructions to start a simultaneous beating of the tom-toms and cans as soon as he judged that I had had time to get round to the other side. I then crept round by myself and soon found a good position and one which the lion was most likely to retreat past, as it was in the middle of a broad animal path leading straight from the place where he was concealed. I lay down behind a small ant hill, and waited expectantly. Very soon I heard a tremendous din being raised by the advancing line of coolies, and almost immediately, to my intense joy, out into the open path stepped a huge maneless lion. It was the first occasion during all these trying months upon which I had had a fair chance at one of these brutes, and my satisfaction at the prospect of bagging him was unbounded.

Slowly he advanced along the path, stopping every few seconds to look round. I was only partially concealed from view, and if his attention had not been so fully occupied by the noise behind him, he must have observed me. As he was oblivious to my presence, however, I let him approach to within about fifteen yards of me, and then covered him with my rifle. The moment I moved to do this, he caught sight of me, and seemed much astonished at my sudden appearance, for he stuck his forefeet into the ground, threw himself back on his haunches and growled savagely. As I covered his brain with my rifle, I felt that at last I had him absolutely at my mercy, but . . . . never trust an untried weapon! I pulled the trigger, and to my horror heard the dull snap that tells of a misfire.

Worse was to follow. I was so taken aback and disconcerted by this untoward accident that I entirely forgot to fire the left barrel, and lowered the rifle from my shoulder with the intention of reloading -- if I should be given time. Fortunately for me, the lion was so distracted by the terrific din and uproar of the coolies behind him that instead of springing on me, as might have been expected, he bounded aside into the jungle again. By this time I had collected my wits, and just as he jumped I let him have the left barrel. An answering angry growl told me that he had been hit; but nevertheless he succeeded once more in getting clear away, for although I tracked him for some little distance, I eventually lost his trail in a rocky patch of ground.

Bitterly did I anathematise the hour in which I had relied on a borrowed weapon, and in my disappointment and vexation I abused owner, maker, and rifle with fine impartiality. On extracting the unexploded cartridge, I found that the needle had not struck home, the cap being only slightly dented; so that the whole fault did indeed lie with the rifle, which I later returned to Farquhar with polite compliments. Seriously, however, my continued ill-luck was most exasperating; and the result was that the Indians were more than ever confirmed in their belief that the lions were really evil spirits, proof against mortal weapons. Certainly, they did seem to bear charmed lives.

After this dismal failure there was, of course, nothing to do but to return to camp. Before doing so, however, I proceeded to view the dead donkey, which I found to have been only slightly devoured it the quarters. It is a curious fact that lions always begin at the tail of their prey and eat upwards towards the head. As their meal had thus been interrupted evidently at the very beginning, I felt pretty sure that one or other of the brutes would return to the carcase at nightfall. Accordingly, as there was no tree of any kind close at hand, I had a staging erected some ten feet away from the body. This machan was about twelve feet high and was composed of four poles stuck into the ground and inclined towards each other at the top, where a plank was lashed to serve as a seat. Further, as the nights were still pitch dark, I had the donkey's carcase secured by strong wires to a neighbouring stump, so that the lions might not be able to drag it away before I could get a shot at them.

At sundown, therefore, I took up my position on my airy perch, and much to the disgust of my gun-bearer, Mahina, I decided to go alone. I would gladly have taken him with me, indeed, but he had a bad cough, and I was afraid lest he should make any

35

involuntary noise or movement which might spoil all. Darkness fell almost immediately, and everything became extraordinarily still. The silence of an African jungle on a dark night needs to be experienced to be realised; it is most impressive, especially when one is absolutely alone and isolated from one's fellow creatures, as I was then. The solitude and stillness, and the purpose of my vigil, all had their effect on me, and from a condition of strained expectancy I gradually fell into a dreamy mood which harmonised well with my surroundings. Suddenly I was startled out of my reverie by the snapping of a twig: and, straining my ears for a further sound, I fancied I could hear the rustling of a large body forcing its way through the bush. "The man-eater," I thought to myself; "surely to-night my luck will change and I shall bag one of the brutes." Profound silence again succeeded; I sat on my eyrie like a statue, every nerve tense with excitement. Very soon, however, all doubt as to the presence of the lion was dispelled. A deep long-drawn sigh -- sure sign of hunger -- came up from the bushes, and the rustling commenced again as he cautiously advanced. In a moment or two a sudden stop, followed by an angry growl, told me that my presence had been noticed; and I began to fear that disappointment awaited me once more.

But no; matters quickly took an unexpected turn. The hunter became the hunted; and instead of either making off or coming for the bait prepared for him, the lion began stealthily to stalk me! For about two hours he horrified me by slowly creeping round and round my crazy structure, gradually edging his way nearer and nearer. Every moment I expected him to rush it; and the staging had not been constructed with an eye to such a possibility. If one of the rather flimsy poles should break, or if the lion could spring the twelve feet which separated me from the ground . . . the thought was scarcely a pleasant one. I began to feel distinctly "creepy," and heartily repented my folly in having placed myself in such a dangerous position. I kept perfectly still, however, hardly daring even to blink my eyes: but the long-continued strain was telling on my nerves, and my feelings may be better imagined than described when about midnight suddenly something came flop and struck me on the back of the head. For a moment I was so terrified that I nearly fell off the plank, as I thought that the lion had sprung on me from behind. Regaining my senses in a second or two, I realised that I had been hit by nothing more formidable than an owl, which had doubtless mistaken me for the branch of a tree -- not a very alarming thing to happen in ordinary circumstances, I admit, but coming at the time it did, it almost paralysed me. The involuntary start which I could not help giving was immediately answered by a sinister growl from below.

After this I again kept as still as I could, though absolutely trembling with excitement; and in a short while I heard the lion begin to creep stealthily towards me. I could barely make out his form as he crouched among the whitish undergrowth; but I saw enough for my purpose, and before he could come any nearer, I took careful aim and pulled the trigger. The sound of the shot was at once followed by a most terrific roar, and then I could hear him leaping about in all directions. I was no longer able to see him, however, as his first bound had taken him into the thick bush; but to make assurance doubly sure, I kept blazing away in the direction in which I heard him plunging about. At length came a series of mighty groans, gradually subsiding into deep sighs, and finally ceasing altogether; and I felt convinced that one of the "devils" who had so long harried us would trouble us no more.

36

As soon as I ceased firing, a tumult of inquiring voices was borne across the dark jungle from the men in camp about a quarter of a mile away. I shouted back that I was safe and sound, and that one of the lions was dead: whereupon such a mighty cheer went up from all the camps as must have astonished the denizens of the jungle for miles around. Shortly I saw scores of lights twinkling through the bushes: every man in camp turned out, and with tom-toms beating and horns blowing came running to the scene. They surrounded my eyrie, and to my amazement prostrated themselves on the ground before me, saluting me with cries of "Mabarak! Mabarak!" which I believe means "blessed one" or "saviour." All the same, I refused to allow any search to be made that night for the body of the lion, in case his companion might be close by; besides, it was possible that he might be still alive, and capable of making a last spring. Accordingly we all returned in triumph to the camp, where great rejoicings were kept up for the remainder of the night, the Swahili and other African natives celebrating the occasion by an especially wild and savage dance.

For my part, I anxiously awaited the dawn; and even before it was thoroughly light I was on my way to the eventful spot, as I could not completely persuade myself that even yet the "devil" might not have eluded me in some uncanny and mysterious way. Happily my fears proved groundless, and I was relieved to find that my luck -- after playing me so many exasperating tricks -- had really turned at last. I had scarcely traced the blood for more than a few paces when, on rounding a bush, I was startled to see a huge lion right in front of me, seemingly alive and crouching for a spring. On looking closer, however, I satisfied myself that he was really and truly stone-dead, whereupon my followers crowded round, laughed and danced and shouted with joy like children, and bore me in triumph shoulder-high round the dead body. These thanksgiving ceremonies being over, I examined the body and found that two bullets had taken effect -- one close behind the left shoulder, evidently penetrating the heart, and the other in the off hind leg. The prize was indeed one to be proud of; his length from tip of nose to tip of tail was nine feet eight inches, he stood three feet nine inches high, and it took eight men to carry him back to camp. The only blemish was that the skin was much scored by the boma thorns through which he had so often forced his way in carrying off his victims.

The news of the death of one of the notorious man-eaters soon spread far and wide over the country: telegrams of congratulation came pouring in, and scores of people flocked from up and down the railway to see the skin for themselves.

## CHAPTER IX

### THE DEATH OF THE SECOND MAN-EATER

It must not be imagined that with the death of this lion our troubles at Tsavo were at an end; his companion was still at large, and very soon began to make us unpleasantly aware of the fact. Only a few nights elapsed before he made an attempt to get at the Permanent Way Inspector, climbing up the steps of his bungalow and prowling round the verandah. The Inspector, hearing the noise and thinking it was a drunken coolie, shouted angrily "Go away!" but, fortunately for him, did not attempt to come out or to open the door. Thus disappointed in his attempt to obtain a meal of human flesh, the lion seized a couple of the Inspector's goats and devoured them there and then.

On hearing of this occurrence, I determined to sit up the next night near the Inspector's bungalow. Fortunately there was a vacant iron shanty close at hand, with a convenient loophole in it for firing from; and outside this I placed three full-grown goats as bait, tying them to a half-length of rail, weighing about 250 lbs. The night passed uneventfully until just before daybreak, when at last the lion turned up, pounced on one of the goats and made off with it, at the same time dragging away the others, rail and all. I fired several shots in his direction, but it was pitch dark and quite impossible to see anything, so I only succeeded in hitting one of the goats. I often longed for a flash-light on such occasions.

Next morning I started off in pursuit and was joined by some others from the camp. I found that the trail of the goats and rail was easily followed, and we soon came up, about a quarter of a mile away, to where the lion was still busy at his meal. He was concealed in some thick bush and growled angrily on hearing our approach; finally, as we got closer, he suddenly made a charge, rushing through the bushes at a great pace. In an instant, every man of the party scrambled hastily up the nearest tree, with the exception of one of my assistants, Mr. Winkler, who stood steadily by me throughout. The brute, however, did not press his charge home: and on throwing stones into the bushes where we had last seen him, we guessed by the silence that he had slunk off. We therefore advanced cautiously, and on getting up to the place discovered that he had indeed escaped us, leaving two off the goats scarcely touched.

Thinking that in all probability the lion would return as usual to finish his meal, I had a very strong scaffolding put up a few feet away from the dead goats, and took up my position on it before dark. On this occasion I brought my gun-bearer, Mahina, to take a turn at watching, as I was by this time worn out for want of sleep, having spent so many nights on the look-out. I was just dozing off comfortably when suddenly I felt my arm seized, and on looking up saw Mahina pointing in the direction of the goats. "Sher!" ("Lion!") was all he whispered. I grasped my double smooth-bore, which, I had charged with slug, and waited patiently. In a few moments I was rewarded, for as I watched the spot where I expected the lion to appear, there was a rustling among the bushes and I saw him stealthily emerge into the open and pass almost directly beneath us. I fired both barrels practically together into his shoulder, and to my joy could see him go down under the force of the blow. Quickly I reached for the magazine rifle, but before I could use it, he was out of sight among the bushes, and I had to fire after him quite at random. Nevertheless I was confident of getting him in the morning, and accordingly set out as soon as it was light. For over a mile there was no difficulty in following the blood-trail, and as he had rested several times I felt sure that he had been badly wounded. In the end, however, my hunt proved fruitless, for after a time the traces of blood ceased and the surface of the ground became rocky, so that I was no longer able to follow the spoor.

About this time Sir Guilford Molesworth, K.C.I.E., late Consulting Engineer to the Government of India for State Railways, passed through Tsavo on a tour of inspection on behalf of the Foreign Office. After examining the bridge and other works and expressing his satisfaction, he took a number of photographs, one or two of which he has kindly allowed me to reproduce in this book. He thoroughly sympathised with us in all the trials we had endured from the man-eaters, and was delighted that one at least was dead. When he asked me if I expected to get the second lion soon, I well remember his half-doubting smile as I rather too confidently asserted that I hoped to bag him also in the course of a few days.

As it happened, there was no sign of our enemy for about ten days after this, and we began to hope that he had died of his wounds in the bush. All the same we still took every precaution at night, and it was fortunate that we did so, as otherwise at least one more victim would have been added to the list. For on the night of December 27, I was suddenly aroused by terrified shouts from my trolley men, who slept in a tree close outside my boma, to the effect that a lion was trying to get at them. It would have been madness to have gone out, as the moon was hidden by dense clouds and it was absolutely impossible to see anything more than a yard in front of one; so all I could do was to fire off a few rounds just to frighten the brute away. This apparently had the desired effect, for the men were not further molested that night; but the man-eater had evidently prowled about for some time, for we found in the morning that he had gone right into every one of their tents, and round the tree was a regular ring of his footmarks.

The following evening I took up my position in this same tree, in the hope that he would make another attempt. The night began badly, as, while climbing up to my perch I very nearly put my hand on a venomous snake which was lying coiled round one of the branches. As may be imagined, I came down again very quickly, but one of my men managed to despatch it with a long pole. Fortunately the night was clear and cloudless, and the moon made every thing almost as bright as day. I kept watch until about 2 a.m., when I roused Mahina to take his turn. For about an hour I slept peacefully with my back to the tree, and then woke suddenly with an uncanny feeling that something was wrong. Mahina, however, was on the alert, and had seen nothing; and although I looked carefully round us on all sides, I too could discover nothing unusual. Only half satisfied, I was about to lie back again, when I fancied I saw something move a little way off among the low bushes. On gazing intently at the spot for a few seconds, I found I was not mistaken. It was the man-eater, cautiously stalking us.

The ground was fairly open round our tree, with only a small bush every here and there; and from our position it was a most fascinating sight to watch this great brute stealing stealthily round us, taking advantage of every bit of cover as he came. His skill showed that he was an old hand at the terrible game of man-hunting: so I determined to run no undue risk of losing him this time. I accordingly waited until he got quite close -- about twenty yards away -- and then fired my .303 at his chest. I heard the bullet strike him, but unfortunately it had no knockdown effect, for with a fierce growl he turned and made off with great long bounds. Before he disappeared from sight, however, I managed to have three more shots at him from the magazine rifle, and another growl told me that the last of these had also taken effect.

We awaited daylight with impatience, and at the first glimmer of dawn we set out to hunt him down. I took a native tracker with me, so that I was free to keep a good look-out, while Mahina followed immediately behind with a Martini carbine. Splashes of blood being plentiful, we were able to get along quickly; and we had not proceeded more than a quarter of a mile through the jungle when suddenly a fierce warning growl was heard right in front of us. Looking cautiously through the bushes, I could see the man-eater glaring out in our direction, and showing his tusks in an angry snarl. I at once took careful aim and fired. Instantly he sprang out and made a most determined charge down on us. I fired again and knocked him over; but in a second he was up once more and coming for me as fast as he could in his crippled condition. A third shot had no apparent effect, so I put out my hand for the Martini, hoping to stop him with it. To my dismay, however, it was not there. The terror of the sudden charge had proved too much for Mahina, and both he and the carbine were by this time well on their way up a tree. In the circumstances there was nothing to do but follow suit, which I did without loss of time: and but for the fact that one of my shots had broken a hind leg, the brute would most certainly have had me. Even as it was, I had barely time to swing myself up out of his reach before he arrived at the foot of the tree.

When the lion found he was too late, he started to limp back to the thicket; but by this time I had seized the carbine from Mahina, and the first shot I fired from it seemed to give him his quietus, for he fell over and lay motionless. Rather foolishly, I at once scrambled down from the tree and walked up towards him. To my surprise and no little alarm he jumped up and attempted another charge. This time, however, a Martini bullet in the chest and another in the head finished him for good and all; he dropped in his tracks not five yards away from me, and died gamely, biting savagely at a branch which had fallen to the ground.

By this time all the workmen in camp, attracted by the sound of the firing, had arrived on the scene, and so great was their resentment against the brute who had killed such numbers of their comrades that it was only with the greatest difficulty that I could restrain them from tearing the dead body to pieces. Eventually, amid the wild rejoicings of the natives and coolies, I had the lion carried to my boma, which was close at hand.

On examination we found no less than six bullet holes in the body, and embedded only a little way in the flesh of the back was the slug which I had fired into him from the scaffolding about ten days previously. He measured nine feet six inches from tip of nose to tip of tail, and stood three feet eleven and a half inches high; but, as in the case of his companion, the skin was disfigured by being deeply scored all over by the boma thorns.

The news of the death of the second "devil" soon spread far and wide over the country, and natives actually travelled from up and down the line to have a look at my trophies and at the "devil-killer", as they called me. Best of all, the coolies who had absconded came flocking back to Tsavo, and much to my relief work was resumed and we were never again troubled by man-eaters. It was amusing, indeed, to notice the change which took place in the attitude of the workmen towards me after I had killed the two lions. Instead of wishing to murder me, as they once did, they could not now do enough for me, and as a token of their gratitude they presented me with a beautiful silver bowl, as well as with a long poem written in Hindustani describing all our trials and my ultimate victory. As the poem relates our troubles in somewhat quaint and biblical language, I have given a translation of it in the appendix. The bowl I shall always consider my most highly prized and hardest won trophy. The inscription on it reads as follows:--

SIR, -- We, your Overseer, Timekeepers, Mistaris and Workmen, present you with this bowl as a token of our gratitude to you for your bravery in killing two man-eating lions at great risk to your own life, thereby saving us from the fate of being devoured by these terrible monsters who nightly broke into our tents and took our fellow-workers from our side. In presenting you with this bowl, we all add our prayers for your long life, happiness and prosperity. We shall ever remain, Sir, Your grateful servants,

Baboo PURSHOTAM HURJEE PURMAR, Overseer and Clerk of Works, on behalf of your Workmen. Dated at Tsavo, January 30, 1899.

Before I leave the subject of "the man-eaters of Tsavo," it may be of interest to mention that these two lions possess the distinction, probably unique among wild animals, of having been specifically referred to in the House of Lords by the Prime Minister of the day. Speaking of the difficulties which had been encountered in the construction of the Uganda Railway, the late Lord Salisbury said:--

"The whole of the works were put a stop to for three weeks because a party of man-eating lions appeared in the locality and conceived a most unfortunate taste for our porters. At last the labourers entirely declined to go on unless they were guarded by an iron entrenchment. Of course it is difficult to work a railway under these conditions, and until we found an enthusiastic sportsman to get rid of these lions, our enterprise was seriously hindered."

Also, The Spectator of March 3, 1900, had an article entitled "The Lions that Stopped the Railway," from which the following extracts are taken:--

"The parallel to the story of the lions which stopped the rebuilding of Samaria must occur to everyone, and if the Samaritans had quarter as good cause for their fears as had the railway coolies, their wish to propitiate the local deities is easily understood. If the whole body of lion anecdote, from the days of the Assyrian Kings till the last year of the nineteenth century, were collated and brought together, it would not equal in tragedy or atrocity, in savageness or in sheer insolent contempt for man, armed or unarmed, white or black, the story of these two beasts.

"To what a distance the whole story carries us back, and how impossible it becomes to account for the survival of primitive man against this kind of foe! For fire -- which has hitherto been regarded as his main safeguard against the carnivora -- these cared nothing. It is curious that the Tsavo lions were not killed by poison, for strychnine is easily used, and with effect. (I may mention that poison was tried, but without effect. The poisoned carcases of transport animals which had died from the bite of the tsetse fly were placed in likely spots, but the wily man-eaters would not touch them, and much preferred live men to dead donkeys.) Poison may have been used early in the history of man, for its powers are employed with strange skill by the men in the tropical forest, both in American and West Central Africa. But there is no evidence that the old inhabitants of Europe, or of Assyria or Asia Minor, ever killed lions or wolves by this means. They looked to the King or chief, or some champion, to kill these monsters for them. It was not the sport but the duty of. Kings, and was in itself a title to be a ruler of men. Theseus, who cleared the roads of beasts and robbers; Hercules, the lion killer; St. George, the dragon-slayer, and all the rest of their class owed to this their everlasting fame. From the story of the Tsavo River we can appreciate their services to man even at this distance of time. When the jungle twinkled with hundreds of lamps, as the shout went on from camp to camp that the first lion was dead, as the hurrying crowds fell prostrate in the midnight forest, laying their heads on his feet, and the Africans danced savage and ceremonial dances of thanksgiving, Mr. Patterson must have realised in no common way what it was to have been a hero and deliverer in the days when man was not yet undisputed lord of the creation, and might pass at any moment under the savage dominion of the beasts."

Well had the two man-eaters earned all this fame; they had devoured between them no less than twenty-eight Indian coolies, in addition to scores of unfortunate African natives of whom no official record was kept.

# CHAPTER X

## THE COMPLETION OF THE TSAVO BRIDGE

When all the excitement had died down and there was no longer any dread of the man-eaters, work went on briskly, and the bridge over the Tsavo rapidly neared completion. As the piers and abutments progressed in height, the question of how to lift the large stones into their positions had to be solved. We possessed no cranes for this purpose, so I set to work and improvised a shears made of a couple of thirty-foot rails. These were bolted together at the top, while the other ends were fixed at a distance of about ten feet apart in a large block of wood. This contrivance acted capitally, and by manipulation of ropes and pulleys the heavy stones were swung into position quickly and without difficulty, so that in a very short time the masonry of the bridge was completed.

The next business was to span the sixty-foot distance between the piers with iron girders. As I had neither winches nor sufficient blocks and tackle to haul these over into position, I was driven to erect temporary piers in the middle of each span, built up crib-shape of wooden sleepers. Great wooden beams were stretched across from the stone piers to these cribs, and laid with rails; and the girder was run over its exact place, while still on the trucks in which it had been brought up from the coast. It was next "jacked" up from the trucks, which were hauled away empty, the temporary bridge was dismantled, and the girder finally lowered gently into position. When the last girder was thus successfully placed, no time was lost in linking up the permanent way, and very soon I had the satisfaction of seeing the first train cross the finished work.

Curiously enough, only a day or so after the bridge had been completed and the intermediate cribs cleared away, a tremendous rain-storm broke over the country. The river started to rise rapidly, soon flooding its banks and becoming a raging murky torrent, tearing up trees by the roots and whirling them along like straws. Steadily higher and higher rose the flood, and standing on my bridge, I watched expectantly for the two temporary trolley bridges -- which, it will be remembered, we had built across the stream in order to bring stone and sand to the main work -- to give way before the ever-rising volume of water. Nor had I long to wait; for I soon caught sight of a solid mass of palm stems and railway sleepers sweeping with almost irresistible force round the bend of the river some little distance above the bridge. This I knew was the debris of the trolley crossing furthest up the river. On it came, and with it an additional bank of stormy-looking water. I held my breath for the space of a moment as it actually leaped at the second frail structure; there was a dull thud and a rending and riving of timbers, and then the flood rolled on towards me, leaving not a vestige of the two bridges behind it. The impact, indeed, was so great that the rails were twisted round the broken tree-trunks as if they had been so much ordinary wire. The double tier of wreckage now swept forward, and hurled itself with a sullen plunge against the cutwaters of my stone piers. The shock was great, but to my immense satisfaction the bridge took it without a tremor, and I saw the remnant of the temporary crossings swirl through the great spans

43

and quickly disappear on its journey to the ocean. I confess that I witnessed the whole occurrence with a thrill of pride.

We were never long without excitement of some kind or another at Tsavo. When the camp was not being attacked by man-eating lions, it was visited by leopards, hyenas, wild dogs, wild cats, and other inhabitants of the jungle around us. These animals did a great deal of damage to the herds of sheep and goats which were kept to supply the commissariat, and there was always great rejoicing when a capture was made in one of the many traps that were laid for them.

Leopards especially are most destructive, often killing simply for pleasure and not for food: and I have always harboured animosity towards them since the night when one wantonly destroyed a whole herd of mine. I happened at the time to have a flock of about thirty sheep and goats which I kept for food and for milk, and which were secured at sundown in a grass hut at one corner of my boma. One particularly dark night we were startled by a tremendous commotion in this shed, but as this was before the man-eaters were killed, no one dared stir out to investigate the cause of the disturbance. I naturally thought that the intruder was one of the "demons," but all I could do was to fire several shots in the direction of the hut, hoping to frighten him away. In spite of these, however, it was some time before the noise died down and everything became still again. As soon as it was dawn I went to the shed to see what had happened, and there, to my intense anger, I found every one of my sheep and goats lying stretched dead, on the ground with its throat bitten through. A hole had been made through the frail wall of the shed, and I saw from this and from the tracks all round that the author of the wholesale slaughter had been a leopard. He had not eaten one of the flock, but had killed them all out of pure love of destruction.

I hoped that he would return the next night to make a meal; and should he do so, I determined to have my revenge. I accordingly left the carcases exactly as they lay, and having a very powerful steel trap -- like an enormous rat-trap, and quite strong enough to hold a leopard if he should put his foot in it -- I placed this in the opening into the shed and secured it by a stout chain to a long stake driven into the ground outside. Darkness found everyone in my boma on the alert and listening anxiously to hear the noise the leopard would make the moment he was caught in the trap. Nor were we disappointed, for about midnight we heard the click of the powerful spring, followed immediately by frantic roaring and plunging. I had been sitting all evening with my rifle by my side and a lantern lighted, so I immediately rushed out, followed by the chaukidar (watchman) carrying the lamp. As we approached the shed, the leopard made a frantic spring in our direction as far as the chain would allow him, and this so frightened the chaukidar that he fled in terror, leaving me in utter darkness. The night was as black as had been the previous one, and I could see absolutely nothing; but I knew the general direction in which to fire and accordingly emptied my magazine at the beast. As far as I could make out, he kept dodging in and out through the broken wall of the goat-house; but in a short time my shots evidently told, as his struggles ceased and all was still. I called out that he was dead, and at once everyone in the boma turned out, bringing all the lanterns in the place. With the others came my Indian overseer, who shouted that he too wanted revenge, as some of the goats had belonged to him. Whereupon he levelled his revolver at the dead leopard, and shutting his eyes tightly, fired four shots in rapid succession. Naturally not one of these touched the beast, but they caused considerable consternation amongst the onlookers, who scattered rapidly to right and left. Next morning a party of starving Wa Kamba happened to be passing just as I was about to skin the leopard, and asked by means of signs to be allowed to do the job for me and then to take the meat. I of course assented to this proposal, and in a very few minutes the skin had been neatly taken off, and the famishing natives began a ravenous meal on the raw flesh.

Wild dogs are also very destructive, and often caused great losses among our sheep and goats. Many a night have I listened to these animals hunting and harrying some poor creature of the wilds round my camp; they never relinquish a chase, and will attack anything, man or beast, when really driven by hunger. I was at Tsavo Station one day -- unfortunately without my rifle -- when one of these dogs came up and stood within about thirty yards of me. He was a fine-looking beast, bigger than a collie, with jet-black hair and a white-tipped bushy tail. I was very sorry that I had not brought my rifle, as I badly wanted a specimen and never had another chance of obtaining one.

## CHAPTER XI

### THE SWAHILI AND OTHER NATIVE TRIBES

I have always been very keenly interested in the different native races of Africa, and consequently availed myself of every opportunity of studying their manners and customs. I had little scope for this at Tsavo, however, as the district around us was practically uninhabited. Still there was of course a good number of Swahili among my workmen, together with a few Wa Kamba, Wa N'yam Wezi, and others, so I soon became more or less acquainted with the habits of these tribes. The Swahili live principally along the coast of British East Africa and at Zanzibar. They are a mixed race, being the descendants of Arab fathers and negro mothers. Their name is derived from the Arabic word suahil, coast; but it has also been said, by some who have found them scarcely so guileless as might have been expected, to be really a corruption of the words sawa hili, that is, "those who cheat all alike." However that may be, the men are as a rule of splendid physique and well qualified for the calling that the majority of them follow, that of caravan porters. They are a careless, light-hearted, improvident people, and are very fond of all the good things of this world, enjoying them thoroughly whenever they get the chance. Their life is spent in journeying to and from the interior, carrying heavy loads of provisions and trade-goods on the one journey, and returning with similar loads of ivory or other products of the country. They are away for many months at a time on these expeditions, and consequently -- as they cannot spend money on the march -- they have a goodly number of rupees to draw on their return to Mombasa. These generally disappear with wonderful rapidity, and when no more fun can be bought, they join another caravan and begin a new safari to the Great Lakes, or even beyond. Many a time have I watched them trudging along the old caravan road which crossed the Tsavo at a ford about half a mile from the railway station: here a halt was always called, so that they might wash and bathe in the cool waters of the river.

Nothing ever seems to damp the spirits of the Swahili porter. Be his life ever so hard, his load ever so heavy, the moment it is off his back and he has disposed of his posho (food), he straightway forgets all his troubles, and begins to laugh and sing and joke with his fellows as if he were the happiest and luckiest mortal alive. Such was my cook, Mabruki, and his merry laugh was quite infectious. I remember that one day he was opening a tin of biscuits for me, and not being able to pull off the under-lid with his fingers, he seized the flap in his magnificent teeth and tugged at it. I shouted to him to stop, thinking that he might break a tooth; but he misunderstood my solicitude and gravely assured me that he would not spoil the tin!

The Swahili men wear a long white cotton garment, like a night-shirt, called a kanzu; the women -- who are too liberally endowed to be entirely graceful -- go about with bare arms and shoulders, and wear a long brightly-coloured cloth which they wind tightly round their bosoms and then allow to fall to the feet. All are followers of the Prophet, and their social customs are consequently much the same as those of any other Mohammedan race, though with a good admixture of savagedom. They have a happy knack of giving a nickname to every European with whom they have to do, such nickname generally making reference to something peculiar or striking in his habits, temper, or appearance. On the whole, they are a kindly, generous folk, whom one cannot help liking.

Of the many tribes which are to be seen about the railway on the way up from the coast, perhaps the most extraordinary-looking are the Wa Nyika, the people who inhabit the thorny nyika (wilderness) which borders on the Taru Desert. They are exceedingly ugly and of a low type. The men wear nothing in the way of dress but a scanty and very dirty cloth thrown over the shoulders, while the women attire themselves only in a short kilt which is tied round them very low at the waist. Both men and women adorn themselves with brass chains round the neck and coils of copper and iron wire round the arms.

The nearest native inhabitants to Tsavo are the Wa Taita, who dwell in the mountains near N'dii, some thirty miles away. My work often took me to this place, and on one of my visits, finding myself with some spare time on my hands, I set out to pay a long promised visit to the District Officer. A fairly good road ran from N'dii Station to his house at the foot of the mountains, about four miles away, and on my arrival I was not only most hospitably entertained but was also introduced to M'gogo, the Head Chief of the Wa Taita, who had just come in for a shauri (consultation) about some affair of State. The old fellow appeared delighted to meet me, and promptly invited me to his kraal, some way up the hills. I jumped at the prospect of seeing the Wa Taita at home, so presently off we started on our heavy climb, my Indian servant, Bhawal, coming with us. After a couple of hours' steady scramble up a steep and slippery goatpath, we arrived at M'gogo's capital, where I was at once introduced to his wives, who were busily engaged in making pombe (a native fermented drink) in the hollowed-out stump of a tree. I presented one of them with an orange for her child, but she did not understand what it was for on tasting it she made a wry face and would not eat it. Still she did not throw it away, but carefully put it into a bag with her other treasures -- doubtless for future investigation. As soon as the women saw Bhawal, however, he became the centre of attraction, and I was eclipsed. He happened to have on a new puggaree, with lots of gold work on it, and this took their fancy immensely; they examined every line most carefully and went into ecstasies over it -- just as their European sisters would have done over the latest Parisian creation.

We made a short halt for rest and refreshment, and then started again on our journey to the top of the hills. After a stiff climb for another two hours, part of it through a thick black forest, we emerged on the summit, where I found I was well rewarded for my trouble by the magnificent views we obtained on all sides. The great Kilima N'jaro stood out particularly well, and made a very effective background to the fine panorama. I was surprised to find a number of well-fed cattle on the mountain top, but I fancy M'gogo thought I was casting an evil spell over them when he saw me taking photographs of them as they grazed peacefully on the sweet grass which covered the plateau.

Like most other natives of Africa, the Wa Taita are exceedingly superstitious, and this failing is turned to good account by the all-powerful "witch-doctor" or "medicine-man." It is, for instance, an extraordinary sight to see the absolute faith with which a Ki Taita will blow the simba-dawa, or "lion medicine ", to the four points of the compass before lying down to sleep in the open. This dawa -- which is, of course, obtainable only from the witch-doctor -- consists simply of a little black powder, usually carried in a tiny horn stuck through a slit in the ear; but the Ki Taita firmly believes that a few grains of this dust blown round him from the palm of the hand is a complete safeguard against raging lions seeking whom they may devour; and after the blowing ceremony he will lie down to sleep in perfect confidence, even in the midst of a man-eater's district. In the nature of things, moreover, he never loses this touching faith in the efficacy of the witch-doctor's charm; for if he is attacked by a lion, the brute sees to it that he does not live to become an unbeliever, while if he is not attacked, it is of course quite clear that it is to the dawa that he owes his immunity.

For the rest, the Wa Taita are essentially a peace-loving and industrious people; and, indeed, before the arrival of the British in the country, they hardly ever ventured down from their mountain fastnesses, owing to their dread of the warlike Masai. Each man has as many wives as he can afford to pay for in sheep or cattle; he provides each spouse with a separate establishment, but the family huts are clustered together, and as a

47

rule all live in perfect harmony. The most curious custom of the tribe is the filing of the front teeth into sharp points, which gives the whole face a most peculiar and rather diabolical expression. As usual, their ideas of costume are rather primitive; the men sometimes wear a scrap of cloth round the loins, while the women content themselves with the same or with a short kilt. Both sexes adorn themselves with a great quantity of copper or iron wire coiled round their arms and legs, and smear their bodies all over with grease, the men adding red clay to the mixture. Many of the women also wear dozens of rows of beads, while their ears are hung with pieces of chain and other fantastic ornaments. The men always carry bows and poisoned arrows, as well as a seemie (a short, roughly-fashioned sword) hung on a leathern thong round the waist. A three-legged stool is also an important part of their equipment, and is slung on the shoulder when on the march.

The next people met with on the road to the Great Lakes are the Wa Kamba, who inhabit the Ukambani province, and may be seen from M'toto Andei to the Athi River. They are a very large tribe, but have little cohesion, being split up, into many clans under chiefs who govern in a patriarchal kind of way. In appearance and dress -- or the want of it -- they are very like the Wa Taita, and they have the same custom of filing the front teeth. As a rule, too, they are a peace-loving people, though when driven to it by hunger they will commit very cruel and treacherous acts of wholesale murder. While the railway was being constructed, a severe famine occurred in their part of the country, when hundreds of them died of starvation. During this period they several times swooped down on isolated railway maintenance gangs and utterly annihilated them, in order to obtain possession of the food which they knew would be stored in the camps. These attacks were always made by night. Like most other native races in East Africa, their only arms are the bow and poisoned arrow, but in the use of these primitive weapons they are specially expert. The arrow-head remains in the flesh when the shaft is withdrawn, and if the poison is fresh, paralysis and death very quickly follow, the skin round the wound turning yellow and mortifying within an hour or two. This deadly poison is obtained, I believe, by boiling down a particular root, the arrow-heads being dipped in the black, pitchy-looking essence which remains. I am glad to say, however, that owing to the establishment of several Mission Stations amongst them, the Wa Kamba are quickly becoming the most civilised natives in the country; and the missionaries have adopted the sensible course of teaching the people husbandry and the practical arts and crafts of everyday life, in addition to caring for their spiritual needs.

# CHAPTER XII

## A NIGHT AFTER HIPPO

During my stay at Tsavo I made many little excursions into the surrounding country, and used to go off on a short shooting and exploring expedition whenever I had the opportunity. I was especially anxious to bag a hippopotamus, so I made up my mind to try my luck on the banks of the Sabaki. Unfortunately, I possessed no heavy rifle, which is almost a necessity for hippo shooting, but it occurred to me to supply the deficiency by manufacturing a few cartridges for my smoothbore. In these I had double charges of powder and a hardened bullet made of lead mixed with about an eighth part of tin. I well remember the anxiety with which I fired the first round of my home-made ammunition. As I more than half expected that the barrel would burst, I lashed the gun in the fork of a tree, tied a piece of string a hundred feet long to the trigger, and then -- taking shelter behind a friendly stump -- pulled off. To my great satisfaction the barrel stood the test perfectly. More than that, on trying the penetrative effect of my bullets, I found that they would smash through a steel plate an eighth of an inch thick at thirty yards' range. This was quite good enough for my purpose, and gave me great confidence in the weapon. All the same, I had a very narrow escape one day while manufacturing some of this ammunition. My plan was to remove the shot from the cartridge, put in the additional powder, and ram this well in before replacing the wad and putting in the bullet. I had clamped my refilling machine to my rough-hewn table, and was stamping the double charge of powder well down into the cartridge, when suddenly, for some unknown reason, the whole charge exploded right into my face. Everything became pitch dark to me, and I groped my way about the little hut in agony of mind as well as of body, for I thought I had been blinded. I am thankful to say, however, that gleams of light soon began to return to my eyes, and in a few hours' time I was almost all right again and able to go on with my cartridge making.

All my preparations having been made, I set out for the Sabaki, taking with me my Indian gun-bearer Mahina, my cook Mabruki, a bhisti (water-carrier), and a couple of natives to carry our odds and ends. On these occasions I usually took no tent, but bivouacked in the open. We took some bread and a few tinned provisions with us, but I could always depend upon getting a paa, guinea-fowl, partridge or rock-rabbit for the larder on the march. These rock-rabbits are more like big rats than rabbits, and are found in great numbers among the rocks along the banks of the rivers. They are not at all bad eating, but the Swahili will not touch them. They call them tupu (shameless, naked things), owing to their lack of a tail, of which indeed they possess not even a vestige.

Our route lay by the always interesting Tsavo River. Along the banks everything within reach of its moisture is delightfully fresh and green. Palms and other trees, festooned with brilliant flowering creepers, flourish along its course; all kinds of monkeys chatter and jabber in the shade overhead as they swing themselves from branch to branch, while birds of the most gorgeous plumage flutter about, giving a very tropical aspect to the scene. On the other hand, if one is tempted to stray away from the river, be it only for a few yards, one comes immediately into the parched, thorny wilderness of stunted, leafless trees. Here the sun beats down pitilessly, and makes the nyika of the Tsavo valley almost intolerable. The river has its source at the foot of snow-crowned Kilima N'jaro, whence it flows for about eighty miles in a northerly direction until it joins the Athi River, about seven miles below Tsavo Station. From this point the united streams take the name of Sabaki and flow more or less eastwards until they reach the Indian Ocean at Malindi, some seventy miles north of Mombasa.

A narrow and tortuous Masai warpath winds along its whole length, but although we followed this trail our journey was nevertheless a very slow one, owing to the overhanging branches and creepers, from which we had constantly to be disengaged. The march was full of interest, however, for it was not long before we came upon fresh tracks both of hippo and rhino. Every now and again, also, we caught glimpses of startled bush-buck and water-buck, while occasionally the sound of a splash in the water told of a wary crocodile. We had gone about half the distance to the Sabaki when we came upon an unexpected obstacle in the shape of a great ridge of barren, rugged rock, about a hundred feet high, which extended for about a mile or so on both banks of the river. The sides of this gorge went sheer down into the water, and were quite impossible to scale. I therefore determined to make a detour round it, but Mahina was confident that he could walk along in the river itself. I hinted mildly at the possibility of there being crocodiles under the rocky ledges. Mahina declared, however, that there was no danger, and making a bundle of his lower garments, he tied it to his back and stepped into the water. For a few minutes all went well. Then, in an instant, he was lifted right off his feet by the rush of the water and whirled away. The river took a sharp bend in this gorge, and he was round it and out of our sight in no time, the last glimpse we caught of him showing him vainly trying to catch hold of an overhanging branch. Although we at once made all the haste we could to get round the ridge of rocks, it took us nearly half an hour to do it. I had almost given up hope of ever seeing Mahina again, and was much relieved, therefore, when we reached the river-side once more, to find him safe and sound, and little the worse for his adventure. Luckily he had been dashed up against a rushy bank, and had managed to scramble out with no more serious damage than a bruised shin.

Eventually we arrived at the junction of the rivers and proceeded some way down the Sabaki, beside which the Tsavo looks very insignificant. Several islands are dotted about in mid-stream and are overgrown with tall reeds and rushes, in which hippo find capital covert all the year round. As with the Tsavo, the banks of the Sabaki are lined with trees of various kinds, affording most welcome shade from the heat of the sun: and skirting the river is a caravan road from the interior -- still used, I believe, for smuggling slaves and ivory to the coast, where dhows are in readiness to convey them to Persia or Arabia.

After an early dinner, which Mabruki soon got ready, I left my followers encamped in a safe boma a mile away from the river, and started out with Mahina to find a suitable

50

tree, near a hippo "run", in which to spend the night. Having some difficulty in finding a likely spot, we crossed to the other side of the river -- rather a risky thing to do on account of the number of crocodiles in it: we found a fairly shallow ford, however, and managed to get safely over. Here, on what was evidently an island during flood time, we found innumerable traces of both hippo and rhino -- in fact the difficulty was to decide which track was the best and freshest. At length I picked out a tree close to the river and commanding a stretch of sand which was all flattened down and looked as if at least one hippo rolled there regularly every night.

As there was still about an hour before sundown, we did not take up our station at once, but proceeded along the bank to see if any other game was about. We had not gone very far when Mahina, who was a little way ahead, signalled to me, and on joining him I saw a splendid-looking water-buck standing in a shallow pool of the river. It was the first time I had seen one of these fine antelope, and I was delighted with the sight. I might have got twenty yards or so nearer, but I thought I had better not risk moving, so I aimed at the shoulder and fired. The buck gave one leap into the air, and then turned and galloped quickly behind an island which completely hid him from view. We waited for him to clear the rushes at the other end of this island, but as he did not appear I got impatient and plunged into the river, regardless of crocodiles or anything else. On rounding the island, however, he was nowhere to be seen, and had evidently turned off while in the shelter of the reeds and so gained the opposite bank. I was keenly disappointed at my failure, for it was impossible to follow him up: to do so we should have had to make a long detour to get across the river, and by that time darkness would have set in. This incident shows the great drawback to the .303 -- namely, that it has very little knock-down effect unless it strikes a vital part; and even then, in a bush country, an animal may manage to go far enough to be lost. On the other hand, an animal wounded with a hard bullet is likely to make a speedy recovery, which is a great blessing.

Mahina was even more upset at the escape of the buck than I was, and as we trudged back through the sand to our tree, he was full of gloomy forebodings of an unlucky night. By the light of a splendid full moon we settled ourselves on a great outspreading branch, and commenced our vigil. Soon the jungle around us began to be alive with its peculiar sounds -- a night bird would call, a crocodile shut his jaws with a snap, or a rhino or hippo crash through the bushes on its way to the water: now and again we could even hear the distant roar of the lion. Still there was nothing to be seen.

After waiting for some considerable time, a great hippo at last made his appearance and came splashing along in our direction, but unfortunately took up his position behind a tree which, in the most tantalising way, completely hid him from view. Here he stood tooting and snorting and splashing about to his heart's content. For what seemed hours I watched for this ungainly creature to emerge from his covert, but as he seemed determined not to show himself I lost patience and made up my mind to go down after him. I therefore handed my rifle to Mahina to lower to me on reaching the ground, and began to descend carefully, holding on by the creepers which encircled the tree. To my intense vexation and disappointment, just as I was in this helpless condition, half-way to the ground, the great hippo suddenly came out from his shelter and calmly lumbered along right underneath me. I bitterly lamented my ill-luck and want of patience, for I could almost have touched his broad back as he passed. It was under these exasperating conditions that I saw a hippo for the first time, and without doubt he is the ugliest and most forbidding looking brute I have ever beheld.

The moment the great beast had passed our tree, he scented us, snorted loudly, and dived into the bushes close by, smashing through them like a traction engine. In screwing myself round to watch him go, I broke the creepers by which I was holding on and landed on my back in the sand at the foot of the tree -- none the worse for my short drop, but considerably startled at the thought that the hippo might come back at any moment. I climbed up to my perch again without loss of time, but he was evidently as much frightened as I was, and returned no more. Shortly after this we saw two rhino come down to the river to drink; they were too far off for a shot, however, so I did not disturb them, and they gradually waddled up-stream out of sight. Then we heard the awe-inspiring roar of a hungry lion close by, and presently another hippo gave forth his tooting challenge a little way down the river. As there seemed no likelihood of getting a shot at him from our tree, I made up my mind to stalk him on foot, so we both descended from our perch and made our way slowly through the trees in the semi-darkness. There were numbers of animals about, and I am sure that neither of us felt very comfortable as we crept along in the direction of the splashing hippo; for my own part I fancied every moment that I saw in front of me the form of a rhino or a lion ready to charge down upon us out of the shadow of the bush.

In this manner, with nerves strung to the highest pitch, we reached the edge of the river in safety, only to find that we were again baulked by a small rush-covered island, on the other side of which our quarry could be heard. There was a good breeze blowing directly from him, however, so I thought the best thing to do was to attempt to get on to the island and to have a shot at him from there. Mahina, too, was eager for the fray, so we let ourselves quietly into the water, which here was quite shallow and reached only to our knees, and waded slowly across. On peering cautiously through the reeds at the corner of the island, I was surprised to find that I could see nothing of the hippo; but I soon realised that I was looking too far ahead, for on lowering my eyes there he was, not twenty-five yards away, lying down in the shallow water, only half covered and practically facing us. His closeness to us made me rather anxious for our safety, more especially as just then he rose to his feet and gave forth the peculiar challenge or call which we had already heard so often during the night. All the same, as he raised his head, I fired at it. He whirled round, made a plunge forward, staggered and fell, and then lay quite still. To make assurance doubly sure, I gave him a couple more bullets as he lay, but we found afterwards that they were not needed, as my first shot had been a very lucky one and had penetrated the brain. We left him where he fell and got back to our perch, glad and relieved to be in safety once more.

As soon as it was daylight we were joined by my own men and by several Wa Kamba, who had been hunting in the neighbourhood. The natives cut out the tusks of the hippo, which were rather good ones, and feasted ravenously on the flesh, while I turned my attention with gratitude to the hot coffee and cakes which Mabruki had meanwhile prepared.

## CHAPTER XIII

### A DAY ON THE N'DUNGU ESCARPMENT

Immediately after breakfast camp was struck, and accompanied by a few of the Wa Kamba, we started off for the N'dungu Escarpment -- a frowning ridge which runs for a great distance parallel to the Sabaki, some three or four miles from its northern bank. We had not gone very far before I caught sight of a fine waterbuck and successfully bowled him over -- a good omen for the day, which put us all in excellent spirits. Mabruki cut off several strips of the tough meat and impaled them on a sharp stick to dry in the sun as he went along. I warned him that he had better be careful that a lion did not scent the meat, as if it did it would be sure to follow up and kill him. Of course I did not mean this seriously; but Mabruki was a great glutton, and by no means courageous, so I wanted to frighten him.

As we trudged along towards the hill, I heard a peculiar noise behind a small rising on our right, and on looking over the crest, I was delighted to see two beautiful giraffe feeding peacefully a little distance away and straining their long necks to get at the tops of some mimosa-like trees, while a young one was lying down in the grass quite close to me. For some time I remained concealed, watching the full-grown pair with great interest: they had evidently just come up from the river, and were slowly making their way back to their home on the escarpment. They seemed on the most affectionate terms, occasionally entwining their great long necks and gently biting each other on the shoulders. Much as I should have liked to have added a giraffe to my collection of trophies, I left them undisturbed, as I think it a pity to shoot these rather rare and very harmless creatures, unless one is required for a special purpose.

We pushed on, accordingly, towards the escarpment, for I was very impatient to get to the top and explore a place where I felt convinced no other white man had ever set foot. From the river the ground rose gently upwards to the foot of the ridge, and was covered more or less densely with stunted trees and bushes, and of course the inevitable "wait-a-bit" thorns. I was fortunate enough, however, to find a rhino path which afforded a fairly comfortable and open road, on which we could walk upright the greater part of the way. The climb up the escarpment itself was a stiff one, and had to be negotiated principally on all-fours, but on the way up I discovered that there was an enormous cleft some miles to the right which would probably have afforded an easier ascent. I had not time to explore it on this particular day, but I made a mental note to do so on some future occasion.

After a two hours' journey from the river we sat panting on the summit after our scramble and surveyed the valley of the Tsavo, which lay spread out like a map about five hundred feet below us. Our home tents, the bridge, Tsavo Station and other buildings were plainly visible, and the railway itself, like a shining snake, could be seen for many miles winding its way through the parched wilderness. Having taken a few photographs of the scene, we turned and struck through the N'dungu Plateau. Here I found the same kind of nyika as that round Tsavo, the only difference being that there were more green trees about. The country, moreover, was somewhat more open, and was intersected by hundreds of broad and well-beaten animal paths, along which we could walk upright in comfort. I was leading the way, followed closely by Mahina and Mabruki, when suddenly we almost walked upon a lion which was lying down at the side of the path and which had probably been asleep. It gave a fierce growl and at once bounded off through the bush; but to Mabruki -- who doubtless recalled then the warning I had given him in fun earlier in the day -- the incident appeared so alarming that he flung down his stick-load of meat and fled for his life, much to the amusement of the others, even the usually silent Wa Kamba joining in the general laughter as they scrambled for the discarded meat. We saw nothing more of the lion, though a few steps further on brought us to the remains of a zebra which he had recently killed and feasted on; but after this Mabruki kept carefully in the rear. Curiously enough, only a short while later we had an exactly similar adventure with a rhino, as owing to the tortuous nature of the path, we walked right into it before we were aware. Like the lion, however, it was more frightened than we, and charged away from us through the jungle.

For about two hours we pursued our journey into the plateau, and saw and heard a wonderful variety of game, including giraffe, rhino, bush-buck, the lesser kudu, zebra, wart-hog, baboons and monkeys, and any number of paa, the last being of a redder colour than those of the Tsavo valley. Of natives or of human habitations, however, we saw no signs, and indeed the whole region was so dry and waterless as to be quite uninhabitable. The animals that require water have to make a nightly journey to and from the Sabaki, which accounts for the thousands of animal paths leading from the plateau to the river.

By this time we were all beginning to feel very tired, and the bhisti's stock of water was running low. I therefore climbed the highest tree I could find in order to have a good look round, but absolutely nothing could I see in any direction but the same flat thorny wilderness, interspersed here and there with a few green trees; not a landmark of any sort or kind as far as the eye could reach; a most hopeless, terrible place should one be lost in it, with certain death either by thirst or by savage beasts staring one in the face. Clearly, then, the only thing to do was to return to the river; and in order to accomplish this before dark it was necessary that no time should be lost. But we had been winding in and out so much through the animal paths that it was no easy matter to say in which direction the Sabaki lay. First I consulted my Wa Kamba followers as to the route back, they simply shook their heads. Then I asked Mahina, who pointed out a direction exactly opposite to that which I felt confident was the right one. Mabruki, of course, knew nothing, but volunteered the helpful and cheering information that we were lost and would all be killed by lions. In these circumstances, I confirmed my own idea as to our way by comparing my watch and the sun, and gave the order to start at once. For two solid hours, however, we trudged along in the fearful heat without striking a single familiar object or landmark. Mabruki murmured loudly; even Mahina expressed grave doubts as to whether the "Sahib" had taken the right direction; only the Wa Kamba stalked along in reassuring silence. For some time we had been following a broad white rhino path, and the great footmarks, of one of these beasts were fresh and plainly visible in the dust. He had been travelling in the opposite direction to us, and I felt sure that he must have been returning from drinking in the river. I accordingly insisted on our keeping to this path, and very soon, to my great relief, we found that we were at the edge of the escarpment, a couple of miles away from the place where we had made the ascent. Here a halt was called; a sheet was spread over some of the stunted trees, and under its shade we rested for half an hour, had some food, and drank the last of our water. After this we pushed on with renewed vigour, and arrived at the Sabaki in good time before sundown, having bagged a couple of guinea-fowl and a paa on the way to serve for dinner. After the long and fatiguing day my bathe in a clear shady pool was a real delight, but I might not have enjoyed it quite so much if I had known then of the terrible fate which awaited one of my followers in the same river the next day. By the time I got back to camp supper was ready and fully appreciated. The tireless Mahina had also collected some dry grass for my bed, and I turned in at once, with my rifle handy, and slept the sleep of the just, regardless of all the wild beasts in Africa.

At dawn Mabruki roused me with a cup of steaming hot coffee and some biscuits, and a start was at once made on our return journey to Tsavo. The place where we had struck the Sabaki the previous evening was some miles further down the stream than I had ever been before, so I decided to take advantage of the Masai trail along its bank until the Tsavo River was reached. I did not think we should meet with any further adventure on our way home, but in the wilds the unexpected is always happening. Shortly after we started one of the Wa Kamba went down to the river's edge to fill his calabash with water, when a crocodile suddenly rose up out of the stream, seized the poor fellow and in a moment had dragged him in. I was on ahead at the time and so did not witness the occurrence, but on hearing the cries of the others I ran back as quickly as possible -- too late, however, to see any sign of either crocodile or native. Mahina philosophically remarked that after all it was only a washenzi (savage), whose loss did not much matter; and the other three Wa Kamba certainly did not appear to be affected by the incident, but calmly possessed themselves of their dead companion's bow and quiver of poisoned arrows, and of the stock of meat which he had left on the bank.

I have since learned that accidents of this kind are of fairly frequent occurrence along the banks of these rivers. On one occasion while I was in the country a British officer had a very lucky escape. He was filling his water bottle at the river, when one of these brutes caught him by the hand and attempted to draw him in. Fortunately one of his servants rushed to his assistance and managed to pull him out of the crocodile's clutches with the loss only of two of his fingers.

As we made our way up the Sabaki, we discovered a beautiful waterfall about a hundred and fifty feet high -- not a sheer drop, but a series of cascades. At this time the river was in low water, and the falls consequently did not look their best; but in flood time they form a fine sight, and the thunder of the falling water can then be plainly heard at Tsavo, over seven miles away, when the wind is in the right direction. We crossed the river on the rocks at the head of these falls, and after some hours' hard marching reached camp without further incident.

## CHAPTER XIV

### THE FINDING OF THE MAN-EATERS' DEN

There were some rocky-looking hills lying to the south-west of Tsavo which I was particularly anxious to explore, so on one occasion when work had been stopped for the day owing to lack of material, I set off for them, accompanied by Mahina and a Punjaubi coolie, who was so stout that he went by the name of Moota (i.e. "Fattie"). In the course of my little excursions round Tsavo I gradually discovered that I was nearly always able to make my way to any required point of the compass by following certain well-defined animal paths, which I mapped out bit by bit during my explorations. On this occasion, for instance, as soon as we had crossed the river and had struck into the jungle, we were fortunate enough to find a rhino path leading in the right direction, which greatly facilitated our progress. As we were making our way along this path through the dry bed of a nullah, I happened to notice that the sandy bottom sparkled here and there where the sunbeams penetrated the dense foliage. This at once filled my head with thoughts of precious stones, and as the spot looked likely enough, I started to dig vigorously at the gravel with my hunting knife. After a few minutes of this work, I came across what I at first took to be a magnificent diamond sparkling in the damp sand: it was about half an inch long, and its facets looked as if they had been cut by an Amsterdam expert. I tested the stone on my watch glass and found that it cut my initials quite easily, and though I knew that quartz would do this as well, it did not seem to me to have either the general appearance or angles of any quartz I had ever seen. For a moment or two I was greatly delighted with my discovery, and began to have rosy dreams of a diamond mine; but I am sorry to say that on closer examination and testing

I was forced to the conclusion that my find was not a diamond, though unlike any other mineral I had ever come across.

My hopes of rapidly becoming a millionaire having thus been dashed to the ground, we proceeded on our way, getting further and further into the depths of a gloomy forest. A little distance on, I noticed through a break in the trees a huge rhino standing in full view near the edge of a ravine. Unfortunately he caught sight of us as well, and before I could take aim, he snorted loudly and crashed off through the tangled undergrowth. As I followed up this ravine, walking stealthily along in the delightful shade of the overhanging palms, I observed on my left a little nullah which opened out of the main channel through a confused mass of jungle and creeper. Through this tangle there was a well-defined archway, doubtless made by the regular passage of rhino and hippo, so I decided to enter and explore what lay beyond. I had not gone very far when I came upon a big bay scooped out of the bank by the stream when in flood and carpeted with a deposit of fine, soft sand, in which were the indistinct tracks of numberless animals. In one corner of this bay, close under an overhanging tree, stood a little sandy hillock, and on looking over the top of this I saw on the other side a fearsome-looking cave which seemed to run back for a considerable distance under the rocky bank. Round the entrance and inside the cavern I was thunderstruck to find a number of human bones, with here and there a copper bangle such as the natives wear. Beyond all doubt, the man-eaters' den! In this manner, and quite by accident, I stumbled upon the lair of these once-dreaded "demons", which I had spent so many days searching for through the exasperating and interminable jungle during the time when they terrorised Tsavo. I had no inclination to explore the gloomy depths of the interior, but thinking that there might possibly still be a lioness or cub inside, I fired a shot or two into the cavern through a hole in the roof. Save for a swarm of bats, nothing came out; and after taking a photograph of the cave, I gladly left the horrible spot, thankful that the savage and insatiable brutes which once inhabited it were no longer at large.

Retracing my steps to the main ravine, I continued my journey along it. After a little while I fancied I saw a hippo among some tall rushes growing on the bank, and quickly signed to Mahina and Moota to stay perfectly still. I then made a careful stalk, only to discover, after all my trouble, that my eyes had deceived me and made me imagine a black bank and a few rushes to be a living animal. We now left the bed of the ravine, and advanced along the top. This turned out to be a good move, for soon we heard the galloping of a herd of some animal or other across our front. I rushed round a corner in the path a few yards ahead, and crouching under the bushes saw a line of startled zebras flying past. This was the first time I had seen these beautifully marked animals in their wild state, so I selected the largest and fired, and as I was quite close to them he dropped in his tracks stone-dead. When I stood over the handsome creature I was positively sorry for having killed him. Not so Moota, however, who rushed up in ecstasy, and before I could stop him had cut his throat. This was done, as he remarked, "to make the meat lawful," for Moota was a devout follower of the Prophet, and no true Mohammedan will eat the flesh of any animal unless the throat has been cut at the proper place and the blood allowed to flow. This custom has often caused me great annoyance, for Mohammedan followers rush in so quickly when an animal is shot and cut the head off so short that it is afterwards quite useless as a trophy.

By the time the zebra was skinned, darkness was fast approaching, so we selected a suitable tree in which to pass the night. Under it we built a goodly fire, made some tea, and roasted a couple of quails which I had shot early in the day and which proved simply delicious. We then betook ourselves to the branches -- at least, Mahina and I did; Moota was afraid of nothing, and said he would sleep on the ground. He was not so full of courage later on, however, for about midnight a great rhino passed our way, winded us and snorted so loudly that Moota scrambled in abject terror up our tree. He was as nimble as a monkey for all his stoutness, and never ceased climbing until he was far above us. We both laughed heartily at his extraordinary haste to get out of danger, and Mahina chaffed him unmercifully.

The rest of the night passed without incident, and in the early morning, while the boys were preparing breakfast, I strolled off towards the rocky hills which I had seen from Tsavo, and which were now only about half a mile distant. I kept a sharp look-out for game, but came across nothing save here and there a paa and a few guinea-fowl, until, just as I was about half-way round the hill, I saw a fine leopard lying on a rocky ledge basking in the morning sun. But he was too quick for me, and made off before I could get a shot; I had not approached noiselessly enough, and a leopard is too wary a beast to be caught napping. Unfortunately I had no more time at my disposal in which to explor these hills, as I was anxious to resume work at Tsavo as soon as possible; so after breakfast we packed up the zebra skin and began to retrace our steps through the jungle. It was an intensely hot day, and we were all very glad when at length we reached the home camp.

Most of my little trips of this sort, however, were made in a northerly direction, towards the ever-interesting Athi or Sabaki rivers. After a long and tiring walk through the jungle what a pleasure it was to lie up in the friendly shelter of the rushes which line the banks, and watch the animals come down to drink, all unconscious of my presence. I took several photographs of scenes of this kind, but unfortunately many of the negatives were spoiled. Often, too, on a brilliant moonlight night have I sat on a rock out in the middle of the stream, near a favourite drinking place, waiting for a shot at whatever fortune might send my way. How exasperating it was, when the wind changed at the critical moment, and gave me away to the rhino or other animal I had sat there for hours patiently awaiting! Occasionally I would get heartily tired of my weary vigil and would wade ashore through the warm water, to make my bed in the soft sand regardless of the snap, snap of the crocodiles which could plainly be heard from the deeper pools up and down the river. At the time, being new to the country, I did not realise the risks I ran; but later on -- after my poor Wa Kamba follower had been seized and dragged under, as I have already described -- I learned to be much more cautious.

The shortest way of reaching the Athi river from Tsavo was to strike through the jungle in a north-westerly direction, and here there was luckily a particularly well-defined rhino path which I always made use of. I discovered it quite by accident on one occasion when I had asked some guests, who were staying with me at Tsavo, to spend a night on the banks of the river. As we were making our way slowly and painfully through the dense jungle, I came across this well-trodden path, which appeared to lead in the direction in which I wished to go, and as I felt convinced that at any rate it would bring us to the river somewhere, I followed it with confidence. Our progress was now easy, and the track led through fairly open glades where traces of bush-buck and water-buck were numerous; indeed once or twice we caught glimpses of these animals as they bounded away to the shelter of the thicket, warned by the sound of our approach. In the end, as I anticipated, the old rhino path proved a true guide, for it struck the Athi at an ideal spot for a camping ground, where some lofty trees close to the bank of the river gave a most grateful and refreshing shade. We had a delightful picnic, and my guests greatly enjoyed their night in the open, although one of them got rather a bad fright from a rhino which suddenly snorted close to our camp, evidently very annoyed at our intrusion on his domain.

In the morning they went off as soon as it was light to try their luck along the river, while I remained in camp to see to breakfast. After an hour or more, however, they all returned, empty-handed but very hungry; so when they had settled down to rest after a hearty meal, I thought I would sally forth and see if I could not meet with better success. I had gone only a short distance up the right bank of the river, when I thought I observed a movement among the bushes ahead of me. On the alert, I stopped instantly, and the next moment was rewarded by seeing a splendid bush-buck advance from the water in a most stately manner. I could only make out his head and neck above the undergrowth, but as he was only some fifty yards off, I raised my rifle to my shoulder to fire. This movement at once caught his eye, and for the fraction of a second he stopped to gaze at me, thus giving me time to aim at where I supposed his shoulder to be. When I fired, he disappeared so suddenly and so completely that I felt sure that I had missed him, and that he had made off through the bush. I therefore re-loaded, and advanced carefully with the intention of following up his trail; but to my unbounded delight I came upon the buck stretched out dead in his tracks, with my bullet through his heart. I lost no time in getting back to camp, the antelope swinging by his feet from a branch borne by two sturdy coolies; and my unlucky friends were very much astonished when they saw the fine bag I had secured in so short a time. The animal was soon skinned and furnished us with a delicious roast for lunch; and in the cool of the evening we made our way back to Tsavo without further adventure.

Some little time after this, while one of these same friends (Mr. C. Rawson) happened to be again at Tsavo, we were sitting after dark under the verandah of my hut. I wanted something from my tent, and sent Meeanh, my Indian chaukidar, to fetch it. He was going off in the dark to do so, when I called him back and told him to take a lantern for fear of snakes. This he did, and as soon as he got to the door of the tent, which was only a dozen yards off, he called out frantically, "Are, Sahib, burra sanp hai!" ("Oh, Master, there is a big snake here!)

"Where?" I shouted.

"Here by the bed," he cried, "Bring the gun, quickly."

59

I seized the shot-gun, which I always kept handy, and rushed to the tent, where, by the light of the lantern, I saw a great red snake, about seven feet long, gazing at me from the side of my camp-bed. I instantly fired at him, cutting him clean in half with the shot; the tail part remained where it was, but the head half quickly wriggled off and disappeared in the gloom of the tent. The trail of blood, however, enabled us to track it, and we eventually found the snake, still full of fight, under the edge of the ground-sheet. He made a last vicious dart at one of the men who had run up, but was quickly given the happy despatch by a blow on the head. Rawson now picked it up and brought it to the light. He then put his foot on the back of its head and with a stick forced open the jaws, when suddenly we saw two perfectly clear jets of poison spurt out from the fangs. An Indian baboo (clerk), who happened to be standing near, got the full benefit of this, and the poor man was so panic-stricken that in a second he had torn off every atom of his clothing. We were very much amused at this, as of course we knew that although the poison was exceedingly venomous, it could do no harm unless it penetrated a cut or open wound in the flesh. I never found out the name of this snake, which, as I have said, was of a dark brick-red colour all over; and I only saw one other of the same kind all the time I was in East Africa. I came upon it suddenly one day when out shooting. It was evidently much startled, and stood erect, hissing venomously; but I also was so much taken aback at its appearance that I did not think about shooting it until it had glided off and disappeared in the thick undergrowth.

## CHAPTER XV

### UNSUCCESSFUL RHINO HUNTS

Although the jungle round Tsavo was a network of rhino paths I had never so far been successful in my efforts to obtain one of these animals, nor was my ambition yet to be realised. One day I was out exploring in the dense bush some six or seven miles away from camp, and found my progress more than usually slow, owing to the fact that I had to spend most of my time crawling on all-fours through the jungle. I was very pleased, therefore, to emerge suddenly on a broad and well-beaten track along which I could walk comfortably in an upright position. In this were some fresh rhino footprints which seemed barely an hour old, so I determined to follow them up. The roadway was beaten in places into a fine white dust by the passage of many heavy animals; and as I pushed cautiously forward I fully expected to come face to face with a rhino at every corner I turned. After having gone a little way I fancied that I really did see one lying at the foot of a tree some distance ahead of me, but on approaching cautiously found that it was nothing more than a great brown heap of loose earth which one of the huge beasts had raised by rolling about on the soft ground. This, however, was evidently a resting-place which was regularly used, so I made up my mind to spend a night in the overhanging branches of the tree.

The next afternoon, accordingly, Mahina and I made our way back to the place, and by dusk we were safely but uncomfortably perched among the branches directly over the path. We had scarcely been there an hour when to our delight we heard a great rhino plodding along the track in our direction. Unfortunately the moon had not yet risen, so I was unable to catch sight of the monster as he approached; I knew, however, that there was light enough for me to see him when he emerged from the bushes into the little clearing round the foot of our tree. Nearer and nearer we heard him coming steadily on, and I had my rifle ready, pointing it in the direction in which I expected his head to appear. But, alas, just at that moment the wind veered round and blew straight from us towards the rhino, who scented us immediately, gave a mighty snort and then dived madly away through the jungle. For some considerable time we could hear him crashing ponderously through everything that came in his way, and he must have gone a long distance before he recovered from his fright and slowed down to his usual pace. At any rate we neither heard nor saw anything more of him, and spent a wakeful and uncomfortable night for nothing.

My next attempt to bag a rhino took place some months later, on the banks of the Sabaki, and was scarcely more successful. I had come down from Tsavo in the afternoon, accompanied by Mahina, and finding a likely tree, within a few yards of the river and with fresh footprints under it, I at once decided to take up my position for the night in its branches. Mahina preferred to sit where he could take a comfortable nap, and wedged himself in a fork of the tree some little way below me, but still some eight or ten feet from the ground. It was a calm and perfect night, such as can be seen only in the tropics; everything looked mysteriously beautiful in the glorious moonlight, and stood out like a picture looked at through a stereoscope. From my perch among the branches I watched first a water-buck come to drink in the river; then a bush-buck; later, a tiny paa emerged from the bushes and paused at every step with one graceful forefoot poised in the air -- thoroughly on the alert and looking round carefully and nervously for any trace of a possible enemy. At length it reached the brink of the river in safety, and stooped to drink. Just then I saw a jackal come up on its trail and begin carefully to stalk it, not even rustling a fallen leaf in its stealthy advance on the poor little antelope. All of a sudden, however, the jackal stopped dead for a second, and then made off out of sight as fast as ever he could go. I looked round to discover the cause of this hurried exit, and to my surprise saw a large and very beautiful leopard crouching down and moving noiselessly in the direction of our tree. At first I thought it must be stalking some animal on the ground below us, but I soon realised that it was Mahina that the brute was intent on. Whether, if left to himself, the leopard would actually have made a spring at my sleeping gun-bearer, I do not know; but I had no intention of letting him have a chance of even attempting this, so I cautiously raised my rifle and levelled it at him. Absolutely noiseless as I was in doing this, he noticed it -- possibly a glint of moonlight on the barrel caught his eye -- and immediately disappeared into the bush before I could get in a shot. I at once woke Mahina and made him come up to more secure quarters beside me.

For a long time after this nothing disturbed our peace, but at last the quarry I had hoped for made his appearance on the scene. Just below us there was an opening in the elephant grass which lined the river's edge, and through this the broad stream shone like silver in the moonlight. Without warning this gap was suddenly filled by a huge black mass -- a rhino making his way, very leisurely, out of the shallow water. On he came with a slow, ponderous tread, combining a certain stateliness with his awkward strides. Almost directly beneath us he halted and stood for an instant clearly exposed to our view. This was my opportunity; I took careful aim at his shoulder and fired. Instantly, and with extraordinary rapidity, the huge beast whirled round like a peg-top, whereupon I fired again. This time I expected him to fall; but instead of that I had the mortification of seeing him rush off into the jungle and of hearing him crash through it like a great steam-roller for several minutes. I consoled myself by thinking that he could not go far, as he was hard hit, and that I should easily find him when daylight arrived. Mahina, who was in a wild state of excitement over the burra janwar (great animal), was also of this opinion, and as there was no longer any reason for silence, he chatted to me about many strange and curious things until the grey dawn appeared. When we got down from our perch, we found the track of the wounded rhino clearly marked by great splashes of blood, and for a couple of miles the spoor could thus be easily followed. At length, however, it got fainter and fainter, and finally ceased altogether, so that we had to abandon the search; the ground round about was rocky, and there was no possibility of telling which way our quarry had gone. I was exceedingly sorry for this, as I did not like to leave him wounded; but there was no help for it, so we struck out for home and arrived at Tsavo in the afternoon very tired, hungry and disappointed.

Rhinos are extraordinary animals, and not in any way to be depended upon. One day they will sheer off on meeting a human being and make no attempt to attack; the next day, for no apparent reason, they may execute a most determined charge. I was told for a fact by an official who had been long in the country that on one occasion while a gang of twenty-one slaves, chained neck to neck as was the custom, was being smuggled down to the coast and was proceeding in Indian file along a narrow path, a rhinoceros suddenly charged out at right angles to them, impaled the centre man on its horns and broke the necks of the remainder of the party by the suddenness of his rush. These huge beasts have a very keen sense of smell, but equally indifferent eyesight, and it is said that if a hunter will only stand perfectly still on meeting a rhino, it will pass him by without attempting to molest him. I feel bound to add, however, that I have so far failed to come across anybody who has actually tried the experiment. On the other hand, I have met one or two men who have been tossed on the horns of these animals, and they described it as a very painful proceeding. It generally means being a cripple for life, if one even succeeds in escaping death. Mr. B. Eastwood, the chief accountant of the Uganda Railway, once gave me a graphic description of his marvellous escape from an infuriated rhino. He was on leave at the time on a hunting expedition in the neighbourhood of Lake Baringo, about eighty miles north of the railway from Nakuru, and had shot and apparently killed a rhino. On walking up to it, however, the brute rose to its feet and literally fell on him, breaking four ribs and his right arm. Not content with

62

this, it then stuck its horn through his thigh and tossed him over its back, repeating this operation once or twice. Finally, it lumbered off, leaving poor Eastwood helpless and fainting in the long grass where he had fallen. He was alone at the time, and it was not for some hours that he was found by his porters, who were only attracted to the spot by the numbers of vultures hovering about, waiting in their ghoulish manner for life to be extinct before beginning their meal. How he managed to live for the eight days after this which elapsed before a doctor could be got to him I cannot imagine; but in the end he fortunately made a good recovery, the only sign of his terrible experience being the absence of his right arm, which had to be amputated.

## CHAPTER XVI

### A WIDOW'S STORY

Very shortly before I left Tsavo I went (on March 11, 1899) on inspection duty to Voi, which, as I have already mentioned, is about thirty miles on the Mombasa side of Tsavo. At this time it was a miserable, swampy spot, where fever, guinea-worm, and all kinds of horrible diseases were rampant; but this state of affairs has now been completely altered by drainage and by clearing away the jungle. Dr. Rose was in medical charge of the place at the time of my visit, and as it was the good old custom to put up with any friend one came across towards nightfall, I made him my host when my day's work was over. We spent a very pleasant evening together, and naturally discussed all the local news. Amongst other things we chatted about the new road which was being constructed from Voi to a rather important missionary station called Taveta, near Mount Kilima N'jaro, and Dr. Rose mentioned that Mr. O'Hara (the engineer in charge of the road-making), with his wife and children, was encamped in the Wa Taita country, about twelve miles away from Voi.

Early next morning I went out for a stroll with my shot-gun, but had not gone far from the doctor's tent when I saw in the distance four Swahili carrying something which looked like a stretcher along the newly-made road. Fearing that some accident had happened, I went quickly to meet them and called out to ask what they were carrying. They shouted back "Bwana" ("The master"); and when I asked what bwana, they replied "Bwana O'Hara." On enquiring what exactly had happened, they told me that during the night their master had been killed by a lion, and that his wife and children were following behind, along the road. At this I directed the men to the hospital and told them where to find Dr. Rose, and without waiting to hear any further particulars hurried

63

on as fast as possible to give what assistance I could to poor Mrs. O'Hara. Some considerable way back I met her toiling along with an infant in her arms, while a little child held on to her skirt, utterly tired out with the long walk. I helped her to finish the distance to the doctor's tent; she was so unstrung by her terrible night's experience and so exhausted by her trying march carrying the baby that she was scarcely able to speak. Dr. Rose at once did all he could both for her and for the children, the mother being given a sleeping draught and made comfortable in one of the tents. When she appeared again late in the afternoon she was much refreshed, and was able to tell us the following dreadful story, which I shall give as nearly as possible in her own words.

"We were all asleep in the tent, my husband and I in one bed and my two children in another. The baby was feverish and restless, so I got up to give her something to drink; and as I was doing so, I heard what I thought was a lion walking round the tent. I at once woke my husband and told him I felt sure there was a lion about. He jumped up and went out, taking his gun with him. He looked round the outside of the tent, and spoke to the Swahili askari who was on sentry by the camp fire a little distance off. The askari said he had seen nothing about except a donkey, so my husband came in again, telling me not to worry as it was only a donkey that I had heard.

The night being very hot, my husband threw back the tent door and lay down again beside me. After a while I dozed off, but was suddenly roused by a feeling as if the pillow were being pulled away from under my head. On looking round I found that my husband was gone. I jumped up and called him loudly, but got no answer. Just then I heard a noise among the boxes outside the door, so I rushed out and saw my poor husband lying between the boxes. I ran up to him and tried to lift him, but found I could not do so. I then called to the askari to come and help me, but he refused, saying that there was a lion standing beside me. I looked up and saw the huge beast glowering at me, not more than two yards away. At this moment the askari fired his rifle, and this fortunately frightened the lion, for it at once jumped off into the bush.

"All four askaris then came forward and lifted my husband back on to the bed. He was quite dead. We had hardly got back into the tent before the lion returned and prowled about in front of the door, showing every intention of springing in to recover his prey. The askaris fired at him, but did no damage beyond frightening him away again for a moment or two. He soon came back and continued to walk round the tent until daylight, growling and purring, and it was only by firing through the tent every now and then that we kept him out. At daybreak he disappeared and I had my husband's body carried here, while I followed with the children until I met you."

Such was Mrs. O'Hara's pitiful story. The only comfort we could give her was to assure her that her husband had died instantly and without pain; for while she had been resting Dr. Rose had made a post-mortem examination of the body and had come to this conclusion. He found that O'Hara had evidently been lying on his back at the time, and that the lion, seizing his head in its mouth, had closed its long tusks through his temples until they met again in the brain. We buried him before nightfall in a peaceful spot close by, the doctor reading the funeral service, while I assisted in lowering the rude coffin into the grave. It was the saddest scene imaginable. The weeping widow, the wondering faces of the children, the gathering gloom of the closing evening, the dusky forms of a few natives who had gathered round -- all combined to make a most striking and solemn ending to a very terrible tragedy of real life.

I am glad to say that within a few weeks' time the lion that was responsible for this tragedy was killed by a poisoned arrow, shot from a tree top by one of the Wa Taita.

## CHAPTER XVII

### AN INFURIATED RHINO

My work at Tsavo was finished in March, 1899, when I received instructions to proceed to railhead and take charge of a section of the work there. For many reasons I was sorry to say good-bye to Tsavo, where I had spent an eventful year; but all the same I was very glad to be given this new post, as I knew that there would be a great deal of interesting work to be done and a constant change of camp and scene, as the line progressed onward to the interior. In good spirits, therefore, I set out for my new headquarters on March 28. By this time railhead had reached a place called Machakos Road, some two hundred and seventy six miles from Mombasa and within a few miles of the great Athi Plains, the latter being treeless and waterless expanses, bare of everything except grass, which the great herds of game keep closely cropped. After leaving Tsavo, the character of the country remains unaltered for some considerable distance, the line continuing to run through the thorny nyika, and it is not until Makindu is reached -- about two hundred miles from the coast -- that a change is apparent. From this place, however, the journey lies through a fairly open and interesting tract of country, where game of all kinds abounds and can be seen grazing peacefully within a few hundred yards of the railway. On the way I was lucky enough to get some fine views of Kilima N'jaro, the whole mountain from base to summit standing out clearly and grandly, with the lofty peak of Kibo topping the fleecy clouds with its snowy head.

At Machakos Road I found the country and the climate very different from that to which I had grown accustomed at Tsavo. Here I could see for miles across stretches of beautiful, open downs, timbered here and there like an English park; and it was a great relief to be able to overlook a wide tract of country and to feel that I was no longer hemmed in on all sides by the interminable and depressing thorny wilderness. As

Machakos Road is some four thousand feet higher above the sea level than Tsavo, the difference in temperature was also very marked, and the air felt fresh and cool compared with that of the sun-baked valley in which I had spent the previous year.

My instructions were to hurry on the construction of the line as fast as possible to Nairobi, the proposed headquarters of the Railway Administration, which lay about fifty miles further on across the Athi Plains; and I soon began to find platelaying most interesting work. Everything has to move as if by clockwork. First the earth surface has to be prepared and rendered perfectly smooth and level; cuttings have to be made and hollows banked up; tunnels have to be bored through hills and bridges thrown across rivers. Then a line of coolies moves along, placing sleepers at regular intervals; another gang drops the rails in their places; yet another brings along the keys, fishplates, bolts and nuts while following these are the men who actually fix the rails on the sleepers and link up from one to another. Finally, the packing gang finishes the work by filling in earth and ballast under and around the steel sleepers to give them the necessary grip and rigidity. Some days we were able to lay only a few yards, while on other days we might do over a mile; all depended on the nature of the country we had to cover. On one occasion we succeeded in breaking the record for a day's platelaying, and were gratified at receiving a telegram of congratulation from the Railway Committee at the Foreign Office.

I made it my custom to take a walk each morning for some distance ahead of rails along the centre-line of the railway, in order to spy out the land and to form a rough estimate of the material that would be required in the way of sleepers, girders for temporary bridges, etc. It was necessary to do this in order to avoid undue delay taking place owing to shortage of material of any kind. About ten days after my arrival at Machakos Road I walked in this way for five or six miles ahead of the last-laid rail. It was rather unusual for me to go so far, and, as it happened, I was alone on this occasion, Mahina having been left behind in camp. About two miles away on my left, I noticed a dark-looking object and thinking it was an ostrich I started off towards it. Very soon, however, I found that it was bigger game than an ostrich, and on getting still nearer made out the form of a great rhinoceros lying down. I continued to advance very cautiously, wriggling through the short grass until at length I got within fifty yards of where the huge beast was resting. Here I lay and watched him; but after some little time he evidently suspected my presence, for rising to his feet, he looked straight in my direction and then proceeded to walk round me in a half-circle. The moment he got wind of me, he whipped round in his tracks like a cat and came for me in a bee-line. Hoping to turn him, I fired instantly; but unfortunately my soft-nosed bullets merely annoyed him further, and had not the slightest effect on his thick hide. On seeing this, I flung myself down quite flat on the grass and threw my helmet some ten feet away in the hope that he would perceive it and vent his rage on it instead of me. On he thundered, while I scarcely dared to breathe. I could hear him snorting and rooting up the grass quite close to me, but luckily for me he did not catch sight of me and charged by a few yards to my left.

As soon as he had passed me, my courage began to revive again, and I could not resist the temptation of sending a couple of bullets after him. These, however, simply cracked against his hide and splintered to pieces on it, sending the dry mud off in little clouds of dust. Their only real effect, indeed, was to make him still more angry. He stood stock-still for a moment, and then gored the ground most viciously and started off once more on the semi-circle round me. This proceeding terrified me more than ever, as I felt sure that he would come up-wind at me again, and I could scarcely hope to escape a second time. Unfortunately, my surmise proved correct, for directly he scented me, up went his nose in the air and down he charged like a battering-ram. I fairly pressed myself into the ground, as flat as ever I could, and luckily the grass was a few inches high. I felt the thud of his great feet pounding along, yet dared not move or look up lest he should see me. My heart was thumping like a steam hammer, and every moment I fully expected to find myself tossed into the air. Nearer and nearer came the heavy thudding and I had quite given myself up for lost, when from my lying position I caught sight, out of the corner of my eye, of the infuriated beast rushing by. He had missed me again! I never felt so relieved in my life, and assuredly did not attempt to annoy him further. He went off for good this time, and it was with great satisfaction that I watched him gradually disappear in the distance. I could not have believed it possible that these huge, ungainly-looking brutes could move so rapidly, and turn and twist in their tracks just like monkeys, had I not actually seen this one do so before my eyes. If he had found me he would certainly have pounded me to atoms, as he was an old bull and in a most furious and vicious mood.

One day when Dr. Brock and I were out shooting, shortly after this incident and not far from where it occurred, we caught sight of two rhinos in a hollow some little distance from us, and commenced to stalk them, taking advantage of every fold of the ground in doing so and keeping about fifty yards apart in case of a charge. In that event one or other of us would be able to get in a broadside shot, which would probably roll the beast over. Proceeding carefully in this manner, we managed to get within about sixty yards of them, and as it was my turn for a shot, I took aim at the larger of the two, just as it was moving its great head from one side to the other, wondering which of us it ought to attack. When at last it decided upon Brock, it gave me the chance I had been waiting for. I fired instantly at the hollow between neck and shoulder; the brute dropped at once, and save for one or two convulsive kicks of its stumpy legs as it lay half on its back, it never moved again. The second rhino proved to be a well-grown youngster which showed considerable fight as we attempted to approach its fallen comrade. We did not want to kill it, and accordingly spent about two hours in shouting and throwing stones at it before at last we succeeded in driving it away. We then proceeded to skin our prize; this, as may be imagined, proved rather a tough job, but we managed it in the end, and the trophy was well worth the pains I had taken to add it to my collection.

# CHAPTER XVIII

## LIONS ON THE ATHI PLAINS

Shortly after I took charge at railhead we entered the Kapiti Plain, which gradually merges into the Athi Plain, and, indeed, is hardly to be distinguished from the latter in the appearance or general character of the country. Together they form a great tract of rolling downs covered with grass, and intersected here and there by dry ravines, along the baked banks of which a few stunted trees -- the only ones to be seen -- struggle to keep themselves alive. In all this expanse there is absolutely no water in the dry season, except in the Athi River (some forty miles away) and in a few water-holes known only to the wild animals. The great feature of the undulating plains, however, and the one which gives them a never-failing interest, is the great abundance of game of almost every conceivable kind. Here I myself have seen lion, rhinoceros, leopard, eland, giraffe, zebra, wildebeeste, hartebeeste, waterbuck, wart-hog, Granti, Thomsoni, impala, besides ostriches, greater and lesser bustard, marabout, and a host of other animals and birds too numerous to name; while along the Athi and close to its banks may be found large numbers of hippo and crocodiles. At the time I was there, these great plains also formed the principal grazing ground for the immense herds of cattle owned by the Masai. I am very glad to say that the whole of this country on the south side of the railway as far as the boundary of German East Africa, from the Tsavo River on the east to the Kedong Valley on the west, is now a strictly protected Game Reserve; and so long, as this huge expanse is thus maintained as a sanctuary, there can be no danger of any of these species becoming extinct.

While crossing this dry expanse, the greatest difficulty I had to contend with was the provision of sufficient water for the three thousand workmen employed about railhead, for not a drop could be obtained on the way, nor could we hope for any until we had got to the other side of the plain and had reached the Athi River, which could not be accomplished under a couple of months. As we progressed onwards into the waterless belt, this became a very serious matter indeed, as any breakdown in the supply would have had the most disastrous consequences among so large a body of men working all day under the blazing sun of a tropical climate. Every day two trainloads of water in great tanks were brought up from the last stream we had passed, which, of course, daily fell further to the rear. This was a source of considerable delay, for the line was blocked all the time the water was being pumped into the tanks, and consequently no material for construction could come through; and a good deal of time was also wasted, when the trains returned to railhead, in distributing the water to the workmen, who often quarrelled and fought in their eagerness to get at it. At first I had most of the tank-filling done by night, but on one occasion a lion came unpleasantly close to the men working the pump, and so night work had to be abandoned. The coolies themselves were so anxious, indeed, to get a plentiful supply of water, that once or twice some of the more daring spirits among them ventured to go out on to the plains in search of waterholes, which, by reason of the large herds of game, we knew must exist somewhere. The only result of these expeditions, however, was that three of these men never returned; what befell them is not known to this day.

When we had proceeded some distance across this dry land, and when I was experiencing to the full the disadvantage and delay caused by my tank trains, a native from some remote corner of the plains -- with nothing by way of dress but a small piece of cowhide thrown over his left shoulder -- came to my tent door one day and squatted down on his heels in the native fashion. On being asked his business, "I have heard," he replied, "that the Great Master wants water; I can show it to him." This was good news, if it could be relied upon; so I questioned him closely, and ascertained that some time previously -- exactly how long ago I could not gather -- he had been in the locality on a raiding expedition and had succeeded in finding water. I asked if the place was far away, and got the reply in Swahili "M'bali kidogo" (" A little distance "). Now, I had had experience of M'bali kidogo before; it is like the Irishman's "mile and a bit." So I decided to start very early next morning on a search for this pond -- for such my informant described it to be. In the meantime the poor fellow, who appeared starving -- there was a sore famine among the natives of the district at the time -- was given food and drink, and made a ravenous meal. In the evening I had a long talk with him in broken Swahili round the camp fire, and obtained some insight into many of the strange and barbarous customs of the Masai, to which interesting tribe he belonged.

In the morning I started off betimes, taking my .303 rifle and being accompanied by Mahina with the 12-bore shot-gun, and by another Indian carrying the necessary food and water. Our Masai guide, whose name we found to be Lungow, seemed to be quite certain of his way, and led us across the rolling plains more or less in the direction in which the railway was to run, but some miles to the right of its centre-line. The march was full of interest, for on the way we passed within easy range of herds of wildebeeste, hartebeeste, gazelle, and zebra. I was out strictly on business, however, and did not attempt a shot, reserving that pleasure for the homeward trip. Late in the forenoon we arrived at Lungow's pond -- a circular dip about eighty yards in diameter, which without doubt had contained water very recently, but which, as I expected to find, was now quite dry. A considerable number of bones lay scattered round it, whether of "kills" or of animals which had died of thirst I could not say. Our guide appeared very much upset when he found the pond empty, and gave vent to many exclamations in his peculiar language, in which the letter "r" rolled like a kettledrum.

Our search for water having thus proved a failure, I determined to try my luck with the game. The Masai and the Indian were sent back to camp, while Mahina and I made a big detour from the dried-up water-hole. Game abounded in all directions, but the animals were much more shy than they had been in the morning, and it was in vain that I stalked -- if it can be called "stalking," when as a matter of fact one has to move in the open -- splendid specimens of Thomson's and Grant's gazelle. I might have attempted a shot once or twice, but the probability was that owing to the long range it would have resulted only in a wound, and I think there is nothing so painful as to see an animal limping about in a crippled condition. In this fruitless manner we covered several miles, and I was beginning to think that we should have to return to camp without so much as

69

firing a shot. Just then, however, I saw a herd of wildebeeste, and with much care managed to get within three hundred yards of them. I singled out the biggest head and waiting for a favourable moment, fired at him, dropping him at once. I ran up to the fallen beast, which appeared to be dying, and told Mahina to drive the hunting knife right through his heart so as to put him quickly out of all pain. As Mahina was not doing this as skilfully or as quickly as I thought it might be done, and seemed unable to pierce the tough hide, I handed him my rifle and took the knife in order to do it myself. Just as I raised the knife to strike, I was startled by the wildebeeste suddenly jumping to his feet. For a moment he stood looking at me in a dazed and tottery kind of way, and then to my amazement he turned and made off. At first he moved with such a shaky and uncertain gait that I felt confident that he could only go a few yards before dropping; so, as I did not wish to disturb the other game around us by firing a second shot, I thought it best just to wait. To my utter astonishment, however, after he had staggered for about sixty yards he seemed to revive suddenly, broke into his ordinary gallop and quickly rejoined the herd. From that time I lost all trace of him, though I followed up for four or five miles.

The wildebeeste, in fact, is like Kipling's Fuzzy-Wuzzy -- "'e's generally shammin' when 'e's dead"; and my friend Rawson about this time had an experience very similar to mine, but attended with more serious results. He had knocked his wildebeeste over in much the same way, and thought it was dead; and as he was very keen on obtaining photographs of game, he took his stand-camera from the Indian who carried it and proceeded to focus it on the animal's head. When he was just about to take the picture, he was thunderstruck to see the wildebeeste jump up and come charging down upon him. He sprang quickly aside, and in an instant up went the camera into the air, followed the next moment by the unfortunate Indian, the wildebeeste having stuck its horn right through the man's thigh and tossed him over its back. Fortunately the brute fell dead after this final effort, leaving Rawson grateful for his escape.

After abandoning the chase of my wildebeeste, we had not gone far on our way towards the home camp when I thought I observed something of a reddish colour moving in a patch of long grass, a good distance to our left front. I asked Mahina if he could make out what it was, but he was unable to do so, and before I could get my field-glasses to bear, the animal, whatever it was, had disappeared into the grass. I kept my eye on the spot, however, and we gradually approached it. When we were about a hundred yards off, the reddish object again appeared; and I saw that it was nothing less than the shaggy head of a lion peeping over the long grass. This time Mahina also saw what it was, and called out, "Dekko, Sahib, sher!" ("Look, Master, a lion!"). I whispered to him to be quiet and to take no notice of him, while I tried my best to follow my own advice. So we kept on, edging up towards the beast, but apparently oblivious of his presence, as he lay there grimly watching us. As we drew nearer, I asked Mahina in a whisper if he felt equal to facing a charge from the sher if I should wound him. He answered simply that where I went, there would he go also; and right well he kept his word.

I watched the lion carefully out of the corner of my eye as we closed in. Every now and then he would disappear from view for a moment; and it was a fascinating sight to see how he slowly raised his massive head above the top of the grass again and gazed calmly and steadily at us as we neared him. Unfortunately I could not distinguish the outline of his body, hidden as it was in the grassy thicket. I therefore circled cautiously round in order to see if the cover was sufficiently thin at the back to make a shoulder shot possible; but as we moved, the lion also twisted round and so always kept his head full on us. When I had described a half-circle, I found that the grass was no thinner and that my chances of a shot had not improved. We were now within seventy yards of the lion, who appeared to take the greater interest in us the closer we approached. He had lost the sleepy look with which he had at first regarded us, and was now fully on the alert; but still he did not give me the impression that he meant to charge, and no doubt if we had not provoked him, he would have allowed us to depart in peace. I, however, was bent on war, in spite of the risk which one must always run by attacking a lion at such close quarters on an open plain as flat as the palm of the hand; so in a standing position I took careful aim at his head, and fired. The distance was, as I have said, a bare seventy yards; yet I must confess to a disgraceful miss. More astonishing still, the beast made not the slightest movement -- did not even blink an eye, so far as I could see -- but continued his steadfast, questioning gaze. Again I took aim, this time for a spot below the tip of his nose, and again I fired -- with more success, the lion turning a complete somersault over his tail. I thought he was done for, but he instantly sprang to his feet again, and to my horror and astonishment was joined by a lioness whose presence we had never even thought of or suspected.

Worse was still to follow, for to our dismay both made a most determined charge on us, bounding along at a great pace and roaring angrily as they came. Poor Mahina cried out, "Sahib, do sher ata hai!" ("Master, two lions are coming!"), but I told him to stand stock-still and for his life not to make the slightest movement. In the twinkling of an eye the two beasts had covered about forty yards of the distance towards us. As they did not show the least sign of stopping, I thought we had given the experiment of remaining absolutely motionless a fair trial, and was just about to raise the rifle to my shoulder as a last resort, when suddenly the wounded lion stopped, staggered, and fell to the ground. The lioness took a couple of bounds nearer to us, and then to my unmeasured relief turned to look round for her mate, who had by this time managed to get to his feet again. There they both stood, growling viciously and lashing their tails, for what appeared to me to be a succession of ages. The lioness then made up her mind to go back to the lion, and they both stood broadside on, with their heads close together and turned towards us, snarling in a most aggressive manner. Had either of us moved hand or foot just then, it would, I am convinced, have at once brought on another and probably a fatal charge.

As the two great brutes stood in this position looking at us, I had, of course, a grand opportunity of dropping both, but I confess I did not feel equal to it at the moment. I could only devoutly hope that they would not renew their attack, and was only too thankful to let them depart in peace if they would, without any further hostility on my part. Just at this juncture the lion seemed to grow suddenly very weak. He staggered some ten yards back towards his lair, and then fell to the ground; the lioness followed, and lay down beside him -- both still watching us, and growling savagely. After a few seconds the lion struggled to his feet again and retreated a little further, the lioness accompanying him until he fell once more. A third time the same thing took place, and at last I began to breathe more freely, as they had now reached the thicket from which they had originally emerged. Accordingly I took a shot at the lioness as she lay beside her mate, partly concealed in the long grass. I do not think I hit her, but anyhow she at once made off and bounded away at a great rate on emerging into the open.

I sent a few bullets after her to speed her on her way, and then cautiously approached the wounded lion. He was stretched out at full length on his side, with his back towards me, but I could see by the heaving of his flanks that he was not yet dead, so I put a bullet through his spine. He never moved after this; but for safety's sake, I made no attempt to go up to him for a few minutes, and then only after Mahina had planted a few stones on his body just to make sure that he was really dead.

We both felt very pleased with ourselves as we stood over him and looked at his fine head, great paws, and long, clean, sharp tusks. He was a young, but full-grown lion in fine condition, and measured nine feet eight and a half inches from tip of nose to tip of tail. My last shot had entered the spine close to the shoulder, and had lodged in the body; the first shot was a miss; as I have already said; but the second had caught him on the forehead, right between the eyes. The bullet, however, instead of traversing the brain, had been turned downwards by the frontal bone, through which it crashed, finally lodging in the root of the tongue, the lead showing on both sides. I cut out the tongue and hung it up to dry, intending to keep it as a trophy; but unfortunately a vulture swooped down when my back was turned, and carried it off.

From the time I knocked the lion over until he first staggered and fell not more than a minute could have elapsed -- quite long enough, however, to have enabled him to cover the distance and to have seized one or other of us. Unquestionably we owed our lives to the fact that we both remained absolutely motionless; and I cannot speak too highly of Mahina for the splendid way in which he stood the charge. Had he acted as did another gun-boy I know of, the affair might not have had so happy an ending. This gun-boy went out with Captain G---- in this very neighbourhood, and not long after our adventure. G---- came across a lion just as we did, and wounded it. It charged down on them, but instead of remaining absolutely still, the terrified gun-boy fled, with the result that the lion came furiously on, and poor G---- met with a terrible death.

While Mahina was scouring the neighbourhood in search of some natives to carry the skin back to camp, I took a good look round the place and found the half-eaten body of a zebra, which I noticed had been killed out in the open and then dragged into the long grass. The tracks told me, also, that all the work had been done by the lion, and this set me thinking of the lioness. I accordingly swept the plain with my glasses in the direction in which she had bounded off, and after some searching I discovered her about a mile away, apparently lying down in the midst of a herd of hartebeeste, who grazed away without taking any notice of her. I felt much inclined to follow her up, but I was afraid that if I did so the vultures that were already hovering around would settle on my lion and spoil the skin, for the destruction of which these ravenous birds are capable, even in the space of only a few minutes, is almost beyond belief. I accordingly returned

72

to the dead beast and sat down astride of him. I had read that a frontal shot at a lion was a very risky one, and on carefully examining the head it was easy to see the reason; for owing to the sharp backward slope of the forehead it is almost impossible for a bullet fired in this manner to reach the brain. As there were lots of lions about in this district and as I wanted to bag some more, I set myself to think out a plan whereby the risk of a frontal shot might be got rid of. About a fortnight afterwards I had an opportunity of putting my scheme into practice, happily with most excellent results; this, however, is another story, which will be told later on.

I next commenced to skin my trophy and found it a very tough job to perform by myself. He proved to be a very fat beast, so I knew that Mahina would make a few honest and well-earned rupees out of him, for Indians will give almost anything for lion fat, believing that it is an infallible cure for rheumatism and various other diseases. When at length the skinning process was completed, I waited impatiently for the return of Mahina, who had by this time been gone much longer than I expected. It is rather a nerve shattering thing -- I am speaking for myself -- to remain absolutely alone for hours on a vast open plain beside the carcase of a dead lion, with vultures incessantly wheeling about above one, and with nothing to be seen or heard for miles around except wild animals. It was a great relief, therefore, when after a long wait I saw Mahina approaching with half-a-dozen practically naked natives in his train. It turned out that he had lost his way back to me, so that it was lucky he found me at all. We lost no time in getting back to camp, arriving there just at sundown, when my first business was to rub wood ashes into the skin and then stretch it on a portable frame which I had made a few days previously. The camp fire was a big one that night, and the graphic and highly coloured description which Mahina gave to the eager circle of listeners of the way in which we slew the lion would have made even "Bahram, that great Hunter," anxious for his fame.

## CHAPTER XIX

### THE STRICKEN CARAVAN

Not long after this adventure the permanent way reached the boundary of the Kapiti Plains, where a station had to be built and where accordingly we took up our headquarters for a week or two. A few days after we had settled down in our new camp, a great caravan of some four thousand men arrived from the interior with luggage and loads of food for a Sikh regiment which was on its way down to the coast, after having been engaged in suppressing the mutiny of the Sudanese in Uganda. The majority of these porters were Basoga, but there were also fair numbers of Baganda (i.e. people of Uganda) and of the natives of Unyoro, and various other tribes. Of course none of these wild men of Central Africa had either seen or heard of a railway in all their lives, and they consequently displayed the liveliest curiosity in regard to it, crowding round one of the engines which happened to be standing at the station, and hazarding the wildest guesses as to its origin and use in a babel of curious native languages. I thought I would provide a little entertainment for them, so I stepped on to the footplate and blew off the steam, at the same time sounding the whistle. The effect was simply magical. The whole crowd first threw themselves flat on the ground howling with fear, and then -- with heads well down and arms well spread out -- they fled wildly in all directions; nor did the stampede cease until I shut off steam and stopped the whistle. Then, their curiosity gradually overpowering them, very cautiously they began to return, approaching the locomotive stealthily as though it were some living monster of the jungle. Eventually, two of their chiefs summoned up courage enough to climb on to the engine, and afterwards thoroughly enjoyed a short run which I had to make down the line in order to bring up some construction material.

Just after this caravan had moved on we were subjected to some torrential rain-storms, which transformed the whole plain into a quaking bog and stopped all railway work for the time being. Indeed, the effect of a heavy downpour of rain in this sun-baked district is extraordinary. The ground, which is of a black sub-soil, becomes a mass of thick mud in no time, and on attempting to do any walking one slides and slips about in the slush in a most uncomfortable manner. Innocent-looking dongas, where half an hour previously not one drop of water was to be seen, become roaring torrents from bank to bank in an incredibly short time; while for many hours or even a few days the rivers become absolutely impassable in this land of no bridges. On this account it is the custom of the wise traveller in these parts always to cross a river before camping, for otherwise a flood may come down and detain him and his caravan on the wrong side of the stream for perhaps a week. Of course when the rain ceases, the floods as quickly subside, the rivers and dongas dry up, and the country once more resumes its normal sun-cracked appearance.

On leaving my tent one morning when work was at a standstill owing to the rain, I noticed a great herd of zebra about a couple of miles away on the north side of the railway. Now, it had long been my ambition to capture one of these animals alive; so I said to myself, "Here is my chance!" The men could do nothing owing to the rain, and the ground was very boggy, so I thought that if we could surround the herd judiciously and chase the zebra up and down from point to point through the heavy ground, some of them would soon get exhausted and we should then be able to catch them. I selected for the hunt a dozen fleet-footed Indians who were employed on the earth works, and who at once entered with great zest into the spirit of the scheme. After having partially surrounded the herd, the half-circle of coolies began to advance with wild shouts, whereupon the zebras galloped madly about from side to side, and then did just what we wished them to do -- made straight for an exceptionally boggy part of the ground, where they soon became more or less helpless. We singled out a few young ones and succeeded in running them to an absolute standstill, when we threw them down and sat on their heads until the other men came up with ropes. In this way we captured no less than six: they were very wild and fractious, giving us a great deal of trouble in getting them along, but eventually we managed to bring them in triumph to the camp, where they were firmly secured. The whole expedition lasted little more than a couple of hours.

Three of the captured zebras I kept for myself, while the other three were given to the Surfacing Engineer, whose men had assisted in the hunt. Two of my three unfortunately died very shortly after; but the third, a sturdy two-year-old, flourished splendidly. At first he was exceedingly vicious, biting and kicking everyone who approached him; indeed, he once planted both his hind feet on my chest, but did me no serious damage beyond throwing me heavily to the ground. In time, however, he became very tame and domesticated, allowing himself to be led about by a rope and head collar, and would drink from a bucket and eat from my hand. He used to be left to graze picketed by a long rope to a stake in the ground; but one afternoon on returning to camp I found, much to my annoyance, that he had disappeared. On making enquiry, I learned from my servants that a herd of wild zebra had galloped close by, and that this had so excited him that he managed to tear the picketing peg out of the ground and so rejoin his brethren in freedom.

Some few days after our successful sortie against the zebra, the great caravan of Basoga porters returned from the coast on their way back to their own country; but alas, with what a terrible difference in their appearance! All their gaiety and lightheartedness was gone, and the poor fellows were in a pitiable state. A frightful epidemic of dysentery had broken out amongst them, doubtless caused by their having eaten food to which they were entirely unaccustomed, their simple diet in their own homes consisting almost entirely of bananas, from which they also make a most refreshing and stimulating drink. The ranks of the caravan were terribly decimated, and dozens of men were left dead or dying along the roadside after each march. It was a case of the survival of the fittest, as of course it was quite impossible for the whole caravan to halt in the wilderness where neither food nor water was to be had. There was only one European with the party, and although he worked like a slave he could do very little among such a number, while the Basoga themselves seemed quite indifferent to the sufferings of their comrades. Thirteen poor wretches fell out to die close to my tent; they were in the most hopeless condition and far too weak to be able to do anything at all for themselves. As soon as I discovered them, I boiled a bucketful of water, added some tins of condensed milk and the greater part of a bottle of brandy to it, and fed them with the mixture. Their feeble cries for some of this nourishment were heartrending; some could only whisper, "Bwana, Bwana" ("Master, Master"), and then open their mouths. One or two of them, indeed, could hardly do even this, and were so weak as to be unable to swallow the spoonful of milk which I put between their lips. In the end six proved to be beyond all help, and died that night; but the remaining seven I managed to nurse into complete recovery in about a fortnight's time. As our camp was moved on, they were brought along from place to place on the top of trucks, until finally they were well enough to resume their journey to Usoga, very grateful indeed for the care which we had taken of them.

75

The day after I first found these stricken natives I had arranged to ride on my pony for some miles in advance of the railway, in order to make arrangements for the building of a temporary bridge over the Stony Athi River -- a tributary of the Athi, and so-called on account of the enormous numbers of stones in its bed and along its banks. I ordered my tent to follow me later in the day, and left directions for the care of the sick Basoga, as I knew I should be away all night. My road lay along the route taken by the home-returning caravan, and every hundred yards or so I passed the swollen corpse of some unfortunate porter who had fallen out and died by the wayside. Before very long I came up with the rearguard of this straggling army, and here I was witness of as unfeeling an act of barbarism as can well be imagined. A poor wretch, utterly unable to go a step further, rolled himself up in his scarlet blanket and lay down by the roadside to die; whereupon one of his companions, coveting the highly-coloured and highly-prized article, turned back, seized one end of the blanket, and callously rolled the dying man out of it as one would unroll a bale of goods. This was too much for me, so I put spurs to my pony and galloped up to the scoundrel, making as if to thrash him with my kiboko, or whip made of rhinoceros hide. In a moment he put his hand on his knife and half drew it from its sheath, but on seeing me dismount and point my rifle at him, he desisted and tried to run away. I made it clear to him by signs, however, that I would fire if he did not at once go back and replace the blanket round his dying comrade. This he eventually did, though sullenly enough, and I then marched him in front of me to the main camp of the caravan, some little distance further on. Here I handed him over to the officer in charge, who, I am glad to say, had him soundly thrashed for his brutality and theft.

After performing this little act of retributive justice, I pushed on towards the Stony Athi. On the way -- while still not far from the caravan camp -- I spied a Grant's gazelle in the distance, and by the aid of my glasses discovered that it was a fine-looking buck with a capital pair of horns. A few Basoga from the caravan had followed me, doubtless in the hope of obtaining meat, of which they are inordinately fond; so, handing them my pony, I wriggled from tuft to tuft and crawled along in the folds of the ground until eventually I got near enough for a safe shot, which bowled the antelope over stone-dead. Scarcely had he dropped when the Basoga swooped down on him, ripped him open, and devoured huge chunks of the raw and still quivering flesh, lapping up the warm blood in the palms of their hands. In return for the meat which I gave them, two of them willingly agreed to go on with me and carry the head and haunch of the gazelle. When we had got very nearly to the place where I intended to camp for the night, a great wart-hog suddenly jumped up almost at my horse's feet, and as he had very fine and exceptionally long tusks, I dismounted at once and bagged him too. The Basoga were delighted at this, and promptly cut off the head; but my own people, who arrived with my tent just at this juncture, and who were all good Mohammedans, were thoroughly disgusted at the sight of this very hideous-looking pig.

I camped for the night on the banks of the Stony Athi, close to where the railway was to cross, and made my notes of what was necessary for the temporary bridge. At the time the river was absolutely dry, but I knew that it might at any moment become a roaring torrent if rain should set in; it would therefore be necessary to span it with a forty-foot girder in order to prevent constant "washouts" during the rainy season. The next morning I started early on my return to railhead. On my way I had to pass the camp which the Basoga caravan had just left, but the spectacle of about a dozen newly-made graves which the hyenas had already torn open caused me to put spurs to my horse and to gallop as fast as possible through the pestilential spot. When I had almost got back to railhead I happened to notice a huge serpent stretched out on the grass, warming himself, his skin of old gold and bright green sparkling brilliantly in the sunshine. He appeared to take little notice of me as I cautiously approached, and was probably drowsy and sated with a heavy meal. I shot him through the head as he lay, and the muscular contortions after death throughout his long body gave me a very vivid idea of the tremendous squeezing power possessed by these reptiles. Skinning him was an easy process, but unfortunately his beautiful colouring soon disappeared, the old gold turning to white and the bright green to lustreless black.

# CHAPTER XX

## A DAY ON THE ATHI RIVER

In spite of all our difficulties, rapid progress continued to be made with the line. Each day railhead crept a mile or so further across the Plains, and on April 24 we reached the Stony Athi River, where our great camp was pitched for a few days while the temporary bridge was being thrown across the dry bed of the stream. Still another temporary bridge had to be arranged for the Athi itself, which was some eight miles further on, so I had to make one or two expeditions to this river in order to select a suitable place for the crossing and to make various other arrangements. On one of these occasions I was busy attending to the pitching of my tent after arriving at the Athi late in the evening, when on looking round I was very much surprised to see two European ladies sitting under the shade of some trees on the river bank. As I knew that this was anything but a safe place in which to rest, owing to the number of lions about, I went up to them to see if I could be of any assistance, and found that they were American missionaries journeying to their stations further inland. They were waiting for their camp equipment to arrive, but their porters had been considerably delayed by some very heavy rain, which of course made the roads bad and the tents about double their usual weight. The men of the party were expected every moment with the porters, but there was as yet no sign of the little caravan, and as a matter of fact it did not arrive until long after nightfall. In these circumstances it was perhaps a great blessing that I happened to be there; and as the ladies were both very tired and hungry, I was glad to be able to place my tent at their disposal and to offer them as good a dinner as it was possible to provide in the wilds. It is indeed wonderful what dangers and hardships these delicately nurtured ladies will face cheerfully in order to carry out their self-appointed mission.

When they had left next morning to resume their journey, I started out and made a search up and down the river for the proper position for my temporary bridge. After a thorough examination of all the possible situations, I chose the most suitable and pitched my tent close to it for a night or two while I made the necessary calculations for carrying out the work. The crossing on which I had decided had to be approached by a somewhat sharp curve in the line, and in laying this out with the theodolite I experienced considerable difficulty, as for some reason or other I could not make the last peg on the curve come anywhere near the tangent point where the curve should link up with the straight. I repeated the whole operation time after time, but always with the same result. Eventually I came to the conclusion that there must be some mistake in the table of angles from which I had been working, so I started to work them out for myself and soon discovered a serious misprint. This being rectified in my calculations, I proceeded to lay out the curve again, when at last everything came out accurately and to my satisfaction.

After I had pegged out this temporary diversion of the line, I thought I richly deserved a few hours' play, and accordingly determined to try my luck after lions up-stream towards the source of the Athi. The river -- which runs almost due north here, before taking a turn eastward to the Indian Ocean -- forms part of the western boundary of the Athi Plains, and is fringed all along its course by a belt of thorny hardwood trees. In some places this fringe is quite narrow, while in others it is about a quarter of a mile wide, with grassy glades here and there among the trees. Every now and again, too, the stream itself widens out into a broad stretch of water, nearly always covered over with tall reeds and elephant grass, while along the banks are frequent patches of stunted bushes, which struck me as very likely places for the king of beasts to sleep in after having drunk at the river. I had noticed that after having eaten and drunk well, a lion would throw himself down quite without caution in the first shady spot he came to; of course nothing except man ever disturbs him, and even of man the lions in this part of the country had as yet no fear, for they had rarely if ever been hunted previous to my time.

As I felt rather tired after my morning's work, I decided to use my pony on this expedition, although as a rule I went on foot. Mahina and half-a-dozen natives to beat the belt of trees were to accompany me, and after a hasty lunch off we started up the left bank of the river. I walked for some distance at first, partly because the ground was very stony and partly because I thought a lion might suddenly bound out of some likely patches in front of the beaters; but after having gone about six miles in this way without adventure of any kind, I decided to mount again. At this time the beaters were in line about a hundred yards behind me, shouting and halloing with all their might as they advanced through the scrub and undergrowth, while I rode well to the flank so as to be ready for any emergency. Just as the men got up to a rather thicker piece of jungle than usual, I fancied I saw a movement among the bushes and pulled up suddenly to watch the spot, but did not dismount. The next moment out bounded a lioness, who raced

78

straight across the open strip into the next patch of jungle, quickly followed by another. Throwing myself off my pony, I seized my rifle to get a shot at the second lioness as she galloped past, and was just about to pull the trigger, when to my utter amazement out sprang a huge black-maned lion, making all haste after his mates. Before he could reach the further thicket, however, I fired, and had the satisfaction of hearing the deep growl that tells of a serious hit.

The beaters and I now advanced with great care, taking advantage of every bit of cover and keeping a sharp look-out for the wounded animal as we crept from tree to tree. Fully a quarter of an hour must have elapsed in this slow yet exciting search, before one of the men, some fifty or sixty yards to my left, and a little ahead of the line, called out that he could see the lion awaiting our approach, with his head just visible in a large bed of rushes only a short distance in front of where I then was. Almost at the same moment I found blood marks left by the wounded animal, leading apparently to a kind of gap in the bank of the river, which had evidently been worn down by a rhino going to and fro to drink. I accordingly made for this with the greatest caution, ordering all the men, except Mahina, to remain behind; and as noiselessly as possible I slipped from cover to cover in my endeavour to obtain a peep over the bank. I saw that it was no use to attempt to climb a tree, as the overspreading foliage would have prevented me from obtaining any view ahead; so I continued my slow advance with a fast-beating heart, not knowing where the huge brute was and expecting every moment that he would charge out at me over the bank from his reedy refuge. Emboldened to a certain extent, however, by the fact that up till then I had heard no movement on the part of my enemy, I crept steadily forward and at last, from the shelter of a friendly tree behind the bole of which I hid myself, I was able to look over the bank. And there, not twenty yards from me, crouched the lion -- luckily watching, not me, but the native who had first seen him and who had directed me to where he was. I raised my rifle very cautiously, without making the slightest sound, and steadying the barrel against the trunk of the tree and standing on tip-toe in order to get a better view, I fired plump at the side of his head. It was as if he had suddenly been hit with a sledgehammer, for he fell over instantly and lay like a log.

On my calling out that the lion was done for, the beaters came running up shouting with joy; and although I warned them to be careful, as the two lionesses were probably still close at hand, they did not seem to care in the slightest and in a twinkling had the dead lion lifted from the reeds on to the dry bank. Before I allowed anything further to be done, however, I had the patch of rushes thoroughly beaten out: but as no traces of the lionesses could be found, we commenced to skin my fine trophy. When this was about half done, I decided to let Mahina finish the operation, while I went on ahead to try my luck either with more lions or with any other game that might come my way. I followed up the river almost to its source, but no more lions crossed my path. Once indeed I felt convinced that I saw one, and gave chase to it with all my might as it rushed through the long grass: but a nearer view showed me nothing more than a huge wart-hog. As I wanted the tusks, which I noticed were very fine ones, I fired but only badly hipped him: so I ran up as fast as I could and at ten yards fired again. This time I missed him entirely, and was puzzled to account for my failure until I looked at my back sight and found that by some accident it had got raised and that I had the 200-yards sight up. On rectifying this, another shot quickly put the wounded animal out of pain.

Still my day's sport was not yet over. While rambling back through the trees I caught sight of a graceful-looking antelope in the distance, and on cautiously approaching closer saw that it was an impala. My stalk was crowned with success, the beautiful animal being bagged without much trouble; and on reaching my prize I was delighted to find that its horns were much above the average. On another occasion I was fortunate enough to get a successful snapshot of an impala just after it had been shot by a friend, and the photograph gives a very good idea of what mine was like.

As it was now growing late, I made all haste back to where I had left Mahina skinning the lion, but to my astonishment he was nowhere to be seen. I fired several shots and shouted myself hoarse, all without response; and the only conclusion I could come to was that he had returned to the camp at the temporary bridge. I accordingly pushed on, reaching home long after dark; and there I found Mahina safe and sound, with the lion's skin already pegged out to dry, so that I could not find it in my heart to give him the severe scolding he deserved for having returned without me. Next morning I packed up my trophies and returned to my work at railhead. On my way back I happened to meet one of the other engineers, who called out, "Hallo! I hear you have got a fine line."

My thoughts being full of my adventures of the day before, I answered: "Yes, I did; but how on earth did you hear of it?"

"Oh!" he said, "Reynolds told me."

"Good heavens," I replied, "why, he left before I shot it."

"Shot?" he exclaimed, "whatever do you mean?"

"Didn't you say," I asked, "that you heard I had got a fine lion?"

"No, no," was his reply; "a fine line for the temporary bridge over the river."

We both laughed heartily at the misunderstanding, and when he saw my trophy, which was being carried by my man just behind me, he agreed that it was quite fine enough to monopolise my thoughts and prevent me from thinking of anything else.

# CHAPTER XXI

## THE MASAI AND OTHER TRIBES

A few Masai may still be seen on the Athi Plains, but as a rule they keep away from the railway, the majority of the tribe being now settled on the Laikipia Plateau. Formerly they were by far the most powerful native race in East Africa, and when on the war-path were the terror of the whole country from the furthest limits of Uganda to Mombasa itself. Their numbers have latterly become greatly reduced through famine and small-pox, but the remnant of the tribe, more especially the men, are still a fine, lithe, clean-limbed people. While I was stationed in the Plains I managed to have an interview with the chief, Lenana, at one of his "royal residences," a kraal near Nairobi. He was affability itself, presenting me with a spear and shield as a memento of the occasion; but he had the reputation of being a most wily old potentate, and I found this quite correct, as whenever he was asked an awkward question, he would nudge his Prime Minister and command him to answer for him. I managed to induce him and his wives and children to sit for their photograph, and they made a very fine group indeed; but unfortunately the negative turned out very badly. I also got Lenana's nephew and a warrior to engage in combat with the spear and shield, and both made fine play with their long keen blades, which more than once penetrated the opponent's shield.

The Masai have a wonderfully well-organised military system. The warriors (elmorani) of the tribe must attend strictly to their duties, and are not allowed to marry or to smoke or to drink until after their term of active service is completed. Besides the spear and shield they generally carry a sword or knobkerrie, suspended from a raw-hide waist-belt; and they certainly look very ferocious in their weird-looking headdress when on the warpath. Once or twice I met detachments out on these expeditions, but they were always quite friendly to me, even though I was practically alone. Before the advent of British rule, however, sudden raids were constantly being made by them on the weaker tribes in the country; and when a kraal was captured all the male defenders-were instantly killed with the spear, while the women were put to death during the night with clubs. The Masai, indeed, never made slaves or took prisoners, and it was their proud boast that where a party of elmorani had passed, nothing of any kind was left alive. The object of these raids was, of course, to capture live stock, for the Masai are not an agricultural people and their wealth consists entirely in their herds of cattle, sheep and goats. Curiously enough they do not hunt game, although the country abounds with it, but live principally on beef and milk; and it is also a common custom for them to drink daily a pint or so of blood taken from a live bullock. As they thus live entirely on cattle, and as cattle cannot thrive without good pasture, it is not unnatural to find that they have a great reverence for grass. They also worship a Supreme Being whom they call N'gai, but this term is also applied to anything which is beyond their understanding.

Perhaps the most curious of the customs of the Masai is the extraction of the two front teeth from the lower jaw. It is said that this habit originated at a time when lockjaw was very prevalent among the tribe, and it was found that if these teeth were pulled out food could still be taken. This explanation seems scarcely satisfactory or sufficient, and I give it only for what it is worth: but whatever the reason for the custom, the absence of these two teeth constitutes a most distinctive identifying mark. I remember once being out with a Masai one day when we came across the bleached skull of a long defunct member of his tribe, of course easily recognisable as such by the absence of the proper teeth. The Masai at once plucked a handful of grass, spat upon it, and then placed it very carefully within the skull; this was done, he said, to avert evil from himself. The same man asked me among many other questions if my country was nearer to God than his. I am afraid I was unable conscientiously to answer him in the affirmative. Formerly the Masai used to spit in the face as a mark of great friendship, but nowadays -- like most other native races -- they have adopted our English fashion of shaking hands.

Another very common custom amongst them is that of distorting the lobe of the ear by stretching it until it hangs down quite five or six inches. It is then pierced and decorated in various ways -- by sticking through it a piece of wood two or three inches in diameter, or a little round tin canister, and by hanging to it pieces of chain, rings, beads, or bunches of brass-headed nails, according to fancy. Nearly all the men wear little bells on their ankles to give notice of their approach, while the women are very fond of covering themselves with large quantities of iron or copper wire. Their limbs, indeed, are often almost completely encased with these rings, which I should think must be very heavy and uncomfortable: but no Masai woman considers herself a lady of fashion without them, and the more she possesses the higher does she stand in the social scale.

As a rule, the Masai do not bury their dead, as they consider this custom to be prejudicial to the soil; the bodies are simply carried some little distance from the village and left to be devoured by birds and wild beasts. The honour of burial is reserved only for a great chief, over whose remains a large mound is also raised. I came across one of these mounds one day near Tsavo and opened it very carefully, but found nothing: possibly I did not pursue my search deep enough into the earth. In general, the Masai are an upright and honourable savage race, and it is a great pity that they are gradually dying out.

More or less serfs of the Masai are the Wa N'derobbo, who, unlike their over-lords, are a race of hunters. They are seldom to be met with, however, as they hide away in caves and thickets, and keep constantly moving from place to place following the game. Not long ago I saw a few of them in the neighbourhood of the Eldama Ravine: but these were more or less civilised, and the girls, who were quite graceful, had abandoned the native undress costume for flowing white robes.

In the district from Nairobi to the Kedong River, and in the Kenya Province, dwell the Wa Kikuyu, who are similar to the Masai in build, but not nearly so good-looking. Like the latter, they use the spear and shield, though of a different shape; their principal weapon, however, is the bow and poisoned arrow. They also frequently carry a rudely made two-edged short sword in a sheath, which is slung round the waist by a belt of raw hide. Their front teeth are filed to a sharp point in the same manner as those of nearly all

82

the other native tribes of East Africa, with the exception of the Masai. They live in little villages composed of beehive huts and always situated in the very thickest patches of forest that they can find, and their cattle kraals are especially strongly built and carefully hidden. On one occasion I managed after a great deal of difficulty and crawling on all-fours to make my way into one of these kraals, and was much amazed to notice what labour and ingenuity had been expended on its construction. Unlike the Masai, the Wa Kikuyu have a fairly good idea of agriculture, and grow crops of m'tama (a kind of native grain from which flour is made), sugar-cane, sweet potatoes, and tobacco.

The Wa Kikuyu have the reputation of being a very cowardly and treacherous people, and they have undoubtedly committed some very cruel deeds. A friend of mine, Captain Haslem, with whom I lived for a few months at Tsavo, was barbarously murdered by some members of this tribe. He left me to go up to the Kikuyu country in charge of the transport, and as he was keenly interested in finding out all about the tropical diseases from which the animals suffered, he made it his custom to dissect the bodies of those that died. The superstitious Wa Kikuyu were fully convinced that by this he bewitched their cattle, which at the time were dying in scores from rinderpest. So -- instigated no doubt by the all-powerful witch-doctor -- they treacherously killed him. For my part, however, I found them not nearly so black as they had been painted to me. I had about four hundred of them working at one thing or another at Nairobi and never had any trouble with them. On the contrary I found them well-behaved and intelligent and most anxious to learn.

As is the case with all other African races, the women of the Wa Kikuyu do the manual labour of the village and carry the heavy loads for their lords and masters, the bundles being held in position on their back by a strap passing round the forehead.

Notwithstanding this some of them are quite pleasant looking, and once they have overcome their fear of the European, do not object to being photographed.

Of the other tribes to be met with in this part of the world, the Kavirondo are the most interesting. They are an industrious, simple people, devoted to agriculture and hospitable in the extreme -- a little addicted to thieving, perhaps, but then that is scarcely considered a sin in the heart of Africa. They are clothed (to use Mark Twain's expression) in little but a smile, a bead or two here and there being considered ample raiment; nevertheless they are modest in their ways and are on the whole about the best of the East African tribes.

# CHAPTER XXII

## HOW ROSHAN KHAN SAVED MY LIFE

On May 12 railhead reached the Athi River, where, as there was a great deal of miscellaneous work to be done, our headquarters remained established for some little time. One day not long after we had settled down in our new camp, I was joined quite unexpectedly by my friend Dr. Brock, who had shared the exciting adventure with me at Tsavo the night we were attacked in the goods-wagon by one of the man-eaters. Now Brock had so far not been fortunate enough to bag a lion, and was consequently most anxious to do so. Shortly after his arrival, accordingly, he suggested that we should go for a shooting expedition on the morrow, and that I should trot out for his benefit one of the local lions. Of course I said I should be delighted -- I was always ready for a hunt when it was possible for me to get away, and as just at the time we were "held up" by the Athi River, I could manage a day off quite easily. So we made the usual preparations for a day's absence from camp -- filled our water-bottles with tea, put a loaf of bread and a tin of sardines in our haversacks, looked carefully to our rifles and ammunition; and warned the "boys" who were to accompany us as beaters to be ready before dawn. I decided to make a very early start, as I knew that the most likely place for lions lay some distance away, and I wanted to get there if possible by daybreak. We should thus have a better chance of catching one of the lords of the plain as he returned from his nightly depredations to the kindly shelter of the tall grass and rushes which fringed the banks of the river. We therefore retired to rest early, and just as I was dozing off to sleep, one of my Indian servants, Roshan Khan, put his head through the slit at my tent door and asked leave to accompany the "Sahibs" in the morning so that he might see what shikar (hunting) was like. This request I sleepily granted, thinking that it could make little difference whether he came with us or stayed behind in camp. As things turned out, however, it made all the difference in the world, for if he had not accompanied us, my shikar would in all probability have ended disastrously next day. He was a very dusky-coloured young Pathan about twenty years of age, lithe and active, and honest and pleasant-looking, as Pathans go. He had been my "boy" for some time and was much attached to me, besides having a touching faith in my prowess in shikar: probably, indeed, this was the reason why he stuck so close to me throughout the hunt.

We breakfasted by candle light and managed to get several miles on our way towards the source of the Athi before dawn. As soon as it was thoroughly daylight, we extended in line, Dr. Brock, as the guest, being placed in the most likely position for a shot, while Roshan Khan followed close behind me with the day's provisions. In this order we trudged steadily forward for a couple of miles without coming across anything, though we advanced through many patches of rushes and long grass likely to conceal our expected quarry. It was most interesting and exciting work all the same, as we never knew but that a lion might the next moment jump up at our very feet. We had just beaten through a most hopeful-looking covert without success and had come out on to a beautiful open grassy glade which stretched away for some distance ahead of us, when I noticed a big herd of wildebeeste browsing quietly some distance to our right. I knew that Brock also wanted a wildebeeste, so I whistled softly to him, and pointed out the weird-looking, bison-like antelopes. He came across at once and started off towards the herd, while I sat down to watch the proceedings. He made a beautiful stalk, which was rendered really very difficult by the open nature of the country, but still the wildebeeste quickly noticed his approach and kept steadily moving on, until at last they disappeared over one of the gentle rises which are such a feature of the Athi Plains.

I still sat and waited, expecting every moment to hear the sound of Brock's rifle. Some time elapsed without a shot, however, and I was just about to follow him up and find out how things were going, when Roshan Khan suddenly exclaimed excitedly:-- " Dekko, Sahib, shenzi ata hain!" ("Look, Sahib, the savages are coming!"). I was not in the least alarmed at this somewhat startling announcement, as the Indians called all the natives of the interior of Africa shenzi, or savages; and on looking round I saw five tall, slim Masai approaching in Indian file, each carrying a six-foot spear in his right hand. On coming nearer, the leader of the party eagerly asked in Swahili, "What does the Bwana Makubwa ("Great Master") desire?"

"Simba" ("Lions"), said I.

"Come," he replied, "I will show you many."

This filled me with interest at once. "How far away are they?" I asked.

"M'bali kidogo" (" A little distance "), came the stereotyped reply.

I immediately had a good look round for Brock, but could see no sign of him, so, in case the "many" lions should get away in the meantime, I told the Masai to lead the way, and off we started.

As usual, the m'bali kidogo proved a good distance -- over two miles in this case. Indeed, I began to get impatient at the long tramp, and called out to the Masai to know where his lions were; but he vouchsafed me no answer and continued to walk steadily on, casting keen glances ahead. After a little I again asked, "Where are the lions?" This time he extended his spear in a most dramatic manner, and pointing to a clump of trees just ahead, exclaimed: "Look, Master; there are the lions." I looked, and at once caught sight of a lioness trotting off behind the bushes. I also saw some suspicious-looking thing at the foot of one of the big trees, but came to the conclusion that it was only a growth of some kind projecting from the trunk. I was soon to be undeceived, however, for as I started to run towards the trees in order to cut off the fast disappearing lioness from a stretch of rushes for which she was making, a low and sinister growl made me look closer at the object which had first aroused my suspicions. To my surprise and delight I saw that it was the head of a huge black-maned lion peering out from behind the trunk of the tree, which completely hid his body. I pulled up short and stared at him.

Although he was not seventy yards away from me, yet owing to the nature of the background it was very difficult to make him out, especially as he kept his head perfectly still, gazing steadily at me. It was only when the great mouth opened in an angry snarl that I could see plainly what he really was. For a few seconds we stood thus and looked at each other; then he growled again and made off after the lioness. As I could not get a fair shot at him from where I stood, I ran with all my might for a point of vantage from which I might have a better chance of bagging him as he passed.

Now by this time I had almost got beyond the surprise stage where lions were concerned; yet I must admit that I was thoroughly startled and brought to a full stop in the middle of my race by seeing no less than four more lionesses jump up from the covert which the lion had just left. In the twinkling of an eye three of them had disappeared after their lord in long, low bounds, but the fourth stood broadside on, looking, not at me, but at my followers, who by this time were grouped together and talking and gesticulating excitedly. This gave me a splendid chance for a shoulder shot at about fifty yards' distance, so I knelt down at once and fired after taking careful aim. The lioness disappeared from sight instantly, and on looking over the top of the grass I saw that my shot had told, as she was on her back, clawing the air and growling viciously. As she looked to me to be done for, I shouted to some of the men to remain behind and watch her, while I set off once more at a run to try to catch up the lion. I feared that the check with the lioness might have lost him to me altogether, but to my relief I soon caught sight of him again. He had not made off very quickly, and had probably stopped several times to see what I was up to; indeed the men, who could see him all the time, afterwards told me that when he heard the growl of rage from the lioness after she was shot, he made quite a long halt, apparently deliberating whether he should return to her rescue. Evidently, however, he had decided that discretion was the better part of valour. Fortunately he was travelling leisurely, and I was delighted to find that I was gaining on him fast; but I had still to run about two hundred yards at my best pace, which, at an altitude of more than 5,000 feet above sea-level, leaves one very breathless at the end of it.

When the lion perceived me running towards him, he took up his station under a tree, where he was half hidden by some low bushes, above which only his head showed. Here he stood, watching my every movement and giving vent to his anger at my presence in low, threatening growls. I did not at all like the look of him, and if there had been another tree close by, I should certainly have scrambled up it into safety before attempting to fire. As a matter of fact, however, there was no shelter of any kind at hand; so, as I meant to have a try for him at all costs, I sat down where I was, about sixty yards from him, and covered his great head with my rifle. I was so breathless after my run, and my arms were so shaky, that it was all I could do to keep the sight on the fierce-looking target and I thought to myself, as the rifle barrel wobbled about, "If I don't knock him over with the first shot, he will be out of these bushes and down on me like greased lightning -- and then I know what to expect." It was a most exciting moment, but in spite of the risk I would not have missed it for the world; so, taking as steady an aim as was possible in the circumstances, I pulled the trigger. Instantly the shaggy head disappeared from view, and such a succession of angry roars and growls came up out of the bushes that I was fairly startled, and felt keenly anxious to finish him off before he could charge out and cover the short distance which separated us. I therefore fired half a dozen shots into the bushes at the spot where I imagined he lay, and soon the growling and commotion ceased, and all was still. I was confident the brute was dead, so I called up one of the men to stay and watch the place, while I again rushed off at full speed -- jumping over such rocks and bushes as came in my way -- to have a shot at a lioness that was still in sight.

By this time my followers numbered about thirty men, as when one is hunting in these plains natives seem to spring from nowhere in the most mysterious manner, and attach themselves to one in the hope of obtaining same portion of the kill. By signal I ordered them to advance in line on the thicket in which the lioness had just taken refuge, while I took up my position on one side, so as to obtain a good shot when she broke covert. The line of natives shouting their native cries and striking their spears together soon disturbed her, and out she sprang into the open, making for a clump of rushes close to the river. Unfortunately she broke out at the most unfavourable spot from my point of view, as some of the natives masked my fire, and I had consequently to wait until she got almost to the edge of the rushes. Whether or not I hit her then I cannot say; at any rate, she made good her escape into the reeds, where I decided to leave her until Brock should arrive.

I now retraced my steps towards the spot where I had shot the lion, expecting, of course, to find the man I had told to watch him still on guard. To my intense vexation, however, I found that my sentry had deserted his post and had joined the other men of the party, having become frightened when left by himself. The result of his disobedience was that now I could not tell where lay the dead lion -- or, rather, the lion which I believed to be dead; but I had no intention of losing so fine a trophy, so I began a systematic search, dividing the jungle into strips, and thus going over the whole place thoroughly. The task of finding him, however, was not so easy as might be thought; the chase after the lioness had taken us some distance from where I had shot him, and as there were numbers of trees about similar to that under which he fell, it was really a very difficult matter to hit upon the right place. At last one of the men sang out joyfully that he had found the lion at the same time running away from the spot as hard as ever he could. A number of those nearest to him, both Indians and natives, had more courage or curiosity, and went up to have a look at the beast. I shouted to them as I hurried along to be careful and not to go too near, in case by any chance he might not be dead; but they paid little heed to the warning, and by the time I got up, some half-dozen of them were gathered in a group at the lion's tail, gesticulating wildly and chattering each in his own language, and all very pleased and excited. On getting near I asked if the lion was dead, and was told that he was nearly so, but that he still breathed. He was lying at full length on his side, and when I saw him at close quarters I was more delighted than I can tell, for he was indeed a very fine specimen. For a moment or two I stood with the group of natives, admiring him. He still breathed regularly, as his flanks heaved with each respiration; but as he lay absolutely still with all the men jabbering within a yard of him, I assumed that he was on the point of death and unable to rise. Possessed with this belief, I very foolishly allowed my curiosity to run away with my caution, and stepped round to have a look at his head. The moment I came into his view, however, he suddenly became possessed of a diabolical ferocity. With a great roar he sprang to his feet, as if he were quite unhurt; his eyes blazed with fury, and his lips were drawn well back, exposing his tusks and teeth in a way I hope never to witness again. When this perilous situation so unexpectedly developed itself, I was not more than three paces away from him.

The instant the lion rose, all the men fled as if the Evil One himself were after them, and made for the nearest trees -- with one exception, for as I took a step backwards, keeping my eye on the infuriated animal, I almost trod on Roshan Khan, who had still remained close behind me. Fortunately for me, I had approached the lion's head with my rifle ready, and as I stepped back I fired. The impact of the .303 bullet threw him back on his haunches just as he was in the act of springing, but in an instant he was up again and coming for me so quickly that I had not even time to raise my rifle to my shoulder, but fired point blank at him from my hip, delaying him for a second or so as before. He was up again like lightning, and again at the muzzle of my rifle; and this time I thought that nothing on earth could save me, as I was almost within his clutches. Help came from an unexpected and unconscious quarter, for just at this critical moment Roshan Khan seemed all at once to realise the danger of the situation, and suddenly fled for his life, screaming and shrieking with all his might. Beyond all question this movement saved me, for the sight of something darting away from him diverted the lion's attention from me, and following his natural instinct, he gave chase instead to the yelling fugitive.

Roshan Khan having thus unwittingly rescued me from my perilous position, it now became my turn to do all I could to save him, if this were possible. In far less time than it takes to tell the story, I had swung round after the pursuing lion, levelled my rifle and fired; but whether because of the speed at which he was going, or because of my over-anxiety to save my "boy", I missed him completely, and saw the bullet raise the dust at the heels of a flying Masai. Like lightning I loaded again from the magazine, but now the lion was within a spring of his prey, and it seemed hopeless to expect to save poor Roshan Khan from his clutches. Just at this moment, however, the terrified youth caught sight of the brute over his left shoulder, and providentially made a quick swerve to the right. As the lion turned to follow him, he came broadside on to me, and just as he had Roshan Khan within striking distance and was about to seize him, he dropped in the middle of what would otherwise assuredly have been the fatal spring -- bowled over with a broken shoulder. This gave me time to run up and give him a final shot, and with a deep roar he fell back full length on the grass, stone-dead.

I then looked round to see if Roshan Khan was all right, as I was not sure whether the lion had succeeded in mauling him or not. The sight that met my eyes turned tragedy into comedy in an instant, and made me roar with laughter; indeed, it was so utterly absurd that I threw myself down on the grass and rolled over and over, convulsed with uncontrollable mirth. For there was Roshan Khan, half-way up a thorn tree, earnestly bent on getting to the very topmost branch as quickly as ever he could climb; not a moment, indeed, was he able to spare to cast a glance at what was happening beneath. His puggaree had been torn off by one thorn, and waved gracefully in the breeze; a fancy waistcoat adorned another spiky branch, and his long white cotton gown was torn to ribbons in his mad endeavour to put as great a distance as possible between himself and the dead lion. As soon as I could stop laughing, I called out to him to come down, but quite in vain. There was no stopping him, indeed, until he had reached the very top of the tree; and even then he could scarcely be induced to come down again. Poor fellow, he had been thoroughly terrified, and little wonder.

My followers now began to emerge from the shelter of the various trees and bushes where they had concealed themselves after their wild flight from the resuscitated lion, and crowded round his dead body in the highest spirits. The Masai, especially, seemed delighted at the way in which he had been defeated, and to my surprise and amusement proved themselves excellent mimics, some three or four of them beginning at once to act the whole adventure. One played the part of the lion and jumped growling at a comrade, who immediately ran backwards just as I had done, shouting "Ta, Ta, Ta" and cracking his fingers to represent the rifle-shots. Finally the whole audience roared with delight when another bolted as fast as he could to Roshan Khan's tree with the pseudo lion roaring after him. At the end of these proceedings up came Brock, who had been attracted to the place by the sound of the firing. He was much astonished to see my fine dead lion lying stretched out, and his first remark was, "You are a lucky beggar!" Afterwards, when he heard the full story of the adventure, he rightly considered me even more lucky than he had first thought.

Our next business was to go back to the lioness which I had first shot and left for dead. Like her mate, however, she was still very much alive when we reached her, so I stalked carefully up to a neighbouring tree, from whose shelter I gave her the finishing shot. We then left Mahina and the other men to skin the two beasts, and went on to the rushes where the second lioness had taken cover. Here all our efforts to turn her out failed, so we reluctantly abandoned the chase and were fated to see no more lions that day.

Our only other adventure was with a stolid old rhino, who gave me rather a fright and induced Brock to indulge in some lively exercise. Separated by about a hundred yards or so, we were walking over the undulating ground a short distance from the river, when, on gaining the top of a gentle rise, I suddenly came upon the ungainly animal as it lay wallowing in a hollow. It jumped to its feet instantly and came for where I stood, and as I had no wish to shoot it, I made a dash for cover round the knoll. On reaching the top of the rise, the rhino winded my companion and at once changed its direction and made for him. Brock lost no time in putting on his best pace in an endeavour to reach the shelter of a tree which stood some distance off, while I sat down and watched the exciting race. I thought it would be a pretty close thing, but felt confident that Brock, who was very active, would manage to pull it off. When he got about half-way to the tree, however, he turned to see how far his pursuer was behind, and in doing so put his foot in a hole in the ground, and to my horror fell head over heels, his rifle flying from his grasp. I expected the great brute to be on him in a moment, but to my intense relief the old rhino stopped dead when he saw the catastrophe which had taken place, and then, failing (I suppose) to understand it, suddenly made off in the opposite direction as hard as he could go. In the meantime Brock had got to his feet again, and

89

raced for dear life to the tree without ever looking round. It was a most comical sight, and I sat on the rise and for the second time that day laughed till my sides ached.

After this we returned to the scene of my morning's adventure, where we found that the invaluable Mahina had finished skinning the two lions. We accordingly made our way back to camp with our trophies, all of us, with perhaps the exception of Roshan Khan, well satisfied with the day's outing. Whenever afterwards I wanted to chaff this "boy", I had only to ask whether he would like to come and see some more shikar. He would then look very solemn, shake his head emphatically and assure me "Kabhi nahin, Sahib" ("Never again, Sir").

## CHAPTER XXIII

### A SUCCESSFUL LION HUNT

When the Athi river had been bridged, the section of the line to Nairobi was pushed forward as rapidly as possible, and from dawn to dark we all exerted ourselves to the very utmost. One day (May 28) the weather was exceptionally hot, and I had been out in the broiling sun ever since daylight superintending the construction of banks and cuttings and the erection of temporary bridges. On returning to my hut, therefore, at about three o'clock in the afternoon, I threw myself into a long deck chair, too tired for anything beyond a long cool drink. Here I rested for an hour or so, amused by the bustle at the small wayside station we had just built, and idly watching our tiny construction engine forging its way, with a great deal of clanking and puffing, up a steep gradient just across the river. It was touch-and-go whether it would manage to get its heavy load of rails and sleepers to the top of the incline or not, and I became so interested in the contest between steam and friction and gravity, that I did not notice that a visitor had approached and was standing quietly beside me.

On hearing the usual salutation, however, I turned round and saw a lean and withered half-bred Masai, clothed in a very inadequate piece of wildebeeste hide which was merely slipped under the left arm and looped up in a knot over the right shoulder. He stood for a moment with the right hand held out on a level with his shoulder, the fingers extended and the palm turned towards me -- all indicating that he came on a friendly visit. I returned his salutation, and asked him what he wanted. Before answering, he dropped down on his heels, his old bones cracking as he did so. "I want to lead the

Great Master to two lions," he said; "they have just killed a zebra and are now devouring it." On hearing this I straightway forgot that I had already done a hard day's work in the full blaze of an equatorial sun; I forgot that I was tired and hungry; in fact, I forgot everything that was not directly connected with the excitement of lion-hunting. Even the old savage at my feet grinned when he saw how keen I was about it. I plied him with questions -- were they both lions or lionesses? had they manes? how far away were they? and so on. Naturally, to the last question he was bound to answer "M'bali kidogo." Of course they were not far away; nothing ever is to a native of East Africa. However, the upshot was that in a very few minutes I had a mule saddled, and with the old Masai as guide, started off accompanied by my faithful Mahina and another coolie to help to bring home the skin if I should prove successful. I also left word for my friend Spooner, the District Engineer, who happened to be absent from camp just at the moment, that I had gone after two lions, but hoped to be back by nightfall.

We travelled at a good pace, and within an hour had covered fully six miles; still there was no sign of lions. On the way we were joined by some Wa Kamba, even more scantily attired than our guide, and soon a dispute arose between these hangers-on and the old Masai, who refused to allow them to accompany us, as he was afraid that they would seize all the zebra-meat that the lions had not already eaten. However, I told him not to bother, but to hurry up and show me the lions, and that I would look after him all right. Eventually, on getting to the low crest of one of the long swells in the ground, our guide extended a long skinny finger and said proudly, "Tazama, Bwana" ("See, Master"). I looked in the direction in which he pointed, and sure enough, about six hundred yards off were a lion and a lioness busily engaged on the carcase of a zebra. On using my field-glasses, I was amused to observe a jackal in attendance on the pair. Every now and then he would come too close to the zebra, when the lion would make a short rush at him and scare him away. The little jackal looked most ridiculous, scampering off before the huge beast with his tail well down; but no sooner did the lion stop and return to his meal than he crept nearer again. The natives say, by the way, that a lion will eat every kind of animal -- including even other lions -- except a jackal or a hyena. I was also interested to notice the way in which the lion got at the flesh of the zebra; he took a short run at the body, and putting his claws well into the skin, in this manner tore off great strips of the hide.

While I was thus studying the picture, my followers became impatient at my inactivity, and coming up to the top of the rise, showed themselves on the sky-line. The lions saw them at once, turning round and standing erect to stare at them. There was not an atom of cover to be seen, nor any chance of taking advantage of the rolling ground, for it did not slope in the required direction; so I started to walk in the open in a sidelong direction towards the formidable-looking pair. They allowed me to come a hundred yards or so nearer them, and then the lioness bolted, the lion following her at a more leisurely trot. As soon as they left the body of the zebra, my African following made a rush for it, and began a fierce fight over the remains, so that I had to restore order and leave a coolie to see that our guide got the large share, as he deserved. In the meantime the lion, hearing the noise of the squabble, halted on the crest of the hill to take a deliberate look at me, and then disappeared over the brow. I jumped on to my mule and galloped as hard as I could after him, and luckily found the pair still in sight when I reached the top of the rise. As soon as they saw me following them up, the lioness took covert in some long grass that almost concealed her when she lay down, but the lion continued to move steadily away. Accordingly I made for a point which would bring me about two hundred yards to the right of the lioness, and which would leave a deep natural hollow between us, so as to give me a better chance, in the event of a charge, of bowling her over as she came up the rise towards me. I could plainly make out her light-coloured form in the grass, and took careful aim and fired. In an instant she was kicking on her back and tossing about, evidently hard hit; in a few seconds more she lay perfectly still, and I saw that she was dead.

I now turned my attention to the lion, who meanwhile had disappeared over another rise. By this time Mahina and the other Indian, with three or four of the disappointed Wa Kamba, had come up, so we started off in a body in pursuit of him. I felt sure that he was lurking somewhere in the grass not far off, and I knew that I could depend upon the native eye to find him if he showed so much as the tip of his ear. Nor was I disappointed, for we had scarcely topped the next rise when one of the Wa Kamba spotted the dark brown head of the brute as he raised it for an instant above the grass in order to watch us. We pretended not to have seen him, however, and advanced to within two hundred yards or so, when, as he seemed to be getting uneasy, I thought it best to risk a shot even at this range. I put up the 200-yards sight and the bullet fell short; but the lion never moved. Raising the sight another fifty yards, I rested the rifle on Mahina's back for the next shot, and again missed; fortunately, however, the lion still remained quiet. I then decided to put into practice the scheme I had thought out the day I sat astride the lion I had killed on the Kapiti Plain: so I told all my followers to move off to the right, taking the mule with them, and to make a half-circle round the animal, while I lay motionless in the grass and waited. The ruse succeeded admirably, for as the men moved round so did the lion, offering me at last a splendid shoulder shot. I took very careful, steady aim and fired, with the result that he rolled over and over, and then made one or two attempts to get up but failed. I then ran up to within a few yards of him, and -- helpless as he was with a bullet through both shoulders -- he was still game, and twist round so as to face me, giving vent all the time to savage growls. A final shot laid him out, however, and we at once proceeded to skin him. While we were busy doing this, one of the Wa Kamba suddenly drew my attention to the fact that we were actually being stalked at that very moment by two other lions, who eventually approached to within five hundred yards' distance and then lay down to watch us skinning their dead brother, their big shaggy heads rising every now and again above the grass to give us a prolonged stare. At the time I little knew what a stirring adventure was in store for me next day while in pursuit of these same brutes.

It was almost dark when the skinning process was finished, so without delay we started on our way back to camp, which was about seven miles off. The lioness I thought I should leave to be skinned the next day; but the men I sent out to do the job on the morrow were unable to find any trace of her -- they probably missed the place where she lay, for I am sure that I killed her. It was a good two hours after night had fallen before we got anywhere near the railway, and the last few miles I was obliged to do by the guidance of the stars. Tramping over the plain on a pitch-dark night, with lions and rhino all about, was by no means pleasant work and I heartily wished myself and my men safely back in camp. Indeed, I was beginning to think that I must have lost my bearings and was getting anxious about it, when to my relief I heard a rifle shot about half a mile ahead of us. I guessed at once that it was fired by my good friend Spooner in order to guide me, so I gave a reply signal; and on getting to the top of the next rise, I saw the plain in front of me all twinkling with lights. When he found that I had not returned by nightfall, Spooner had become nervous about me, and fearing that I had met with some mishap, had come out with a number of the workmen in camp to search for me in the direction I had taken in the afternoon. He was delighted to find me safe and sound and with a lion's skin as a trophy, while I was equally glad to have his escort and company back to camp, which was still over a mile away.

When we had settled down comfortably to dinner that night, I fired Spooner's sporting ardour by telling him of the fine pair of lions who had watched us skinning their companion, and we agreed at once to go out next day and try to bag them both. Spooner and I had often had many friendly arguments in regard to the comparative courage of the lion and the tiger, he holding the view that "Stripes" was the more formidable foe, while I, though admitting to the full-the courage of the tiger, maintained from lively personal experience that the lion when once roused was unequalled for pluck and daring, and was in fact the most dangerous enemy one could meet with. He may at times slink off and not show fight; but get him in the mood, or wound him, and only his death or yours will end the fray -- that, at least, was my experience of East African lions. I think that Spooner has now come round to my opinion, his conversion taking place the next day in a very melancholy manner.

## CHAPTER XXIV

### BHOOTA'S LAST SHIKAR

Long after I had retired to rest that night I lay awake listening to roar answering roar in every direction round our camp, and realised that we were indeed in the midst of a favourite haunt of the king of beasts. It is one thing to hear a lion in captivity, when one knows he is safe behind iron bars; but quite another to listen to him when he is ramping around in the vicinity of one's fragile tent, which with a single blow he could tear to pieces. Still, all this roaring was of good omen for the next day's sport.

According to our over-night arrangement, we were up betimes in the morning, but as there was a great deal of work to be done before we could get away, it was quite midday before we made ready to start. I ought to mention before going further that as a rule Spooner declined my company on shooting trips, as he was convinced that I should get "scuppered" sooner or later if I persisted in going after lions with a "popgun," as he contemptuously termed my .303. Indeed, this was rather a bone of contention between us, he being a firm believer (and rightly) in a heavy, weapon for big and dangerous game, while I always did my best to defend the .303 which I was in the habit of using. On this occasion we effected a compromise for the day, I accepting the loan of his spare 12-bore rifle as a second gun in case I should get to close quarters. But my experience has been that it is always a very dangerous thing to rely on a borrowed gun or rifle, unless it has precisely the same action as one's own; and certainly in this instance it almost proved disastrous.

Having thus seen to our rifles and ammunition and taken care also that some brandy was put in the luncheon-basket in case of an accident, we set off early in the afternoon in Spooner's tonga, which is a two-wheeled cart with a hood over it. The party consisted of Spooner and myself, Spooner's Indian shikari Bhoota, my own gun-boy Mahina, and two other Indians, one of whom, Imam Din, rode in the tonga, while the other led a spare horse called "Blazeaway." Now it may seem a strange plan to go lion-hunting in a tonga, but there is no better way of getting about country like the Athi Plains, where -- so long as it is dry -- there is little or nothing to obstruct wheeled traffic. Once started, we rattled over the smooth expanse at a good rate, and on the way bagged a hartebeeste and a couple of gazelle, as fresh meat was badly needed in camp; besides, they offered most tempting shots, for they stood stock-still gazing at us, struck no doubt by the novel appearance of our conveyance. Next we came upon a herd of wildebeeste, and here we allowed Bhoota, who was a wary shikari and an old servant of Spooner's, to stalk a solitary bull. He was highly pleased at this favour, and did the job admirably.

At last we reached the spot where I had seen the two lions on the previous day -- a slight hollow, covered with long grass; but there was now no trace of them to be discovered, so we moved further on and had another good beat round. After some little time the excitement began by our spying the black-tipped ears of a lioness projecting above the grass, and the next moment a very fine lion arose from beside her and gave us a full view of his grand head and mane. After staring fixedly at us in an inquiring sort of way as we slowly advanced upon them, they both turned and slowly trotted off, the lion stopping every now and again to gaze round in our direction. Very imposing and majestic he looked, too, as he thus turned his great shaggy head defiantly towards us, and Spooner had to admit that it was the finest sight he had ever seen. For a while we followed them on foot; but finding at length that they were getting away from us and would soon be lost to sight over a bit of rising ground, we jumped quickly into the tonga and galloped round the base of the knoll so as to cut off their retreat, the excitement of the rough and bumpy ride being intensified a hundred-fold by the probability of our driving slap into the pair on rounding the rise. On getting to the other side, however, they were nowhere to be seen, so we drove on as hard as we could to the top, whence we caught sight of them about four hundred yards away. As there seemed to be no prospect of getting nearer we decided to open fire at this range, and at the third shot the lioness tumbled over to my .303. At first I thought I had done for her, as for a few minutes she lay on the ground kicking and struggling; but in the end, although evidently badly hit, she rose to her feet and followed the lion, who had escaped uninjured, into some long grass from which we could not hope to dislodge them.

As it was now late in the afternoon, and as there seemed no possibility of inducing the lions to leave the thicket in which they had concealed themselves, we turned back towards camp, intending to come out again the next day to track the wounded lioness. I was now riding "Blazeaway" and was trotting along in advance of the tonga, when suddenly he shied badly at a hyena, which sprang up out of the grass almost from beneath his feet and quickly scampered off. I pulled up for a moment and sat watching the hyena's ungainly bounds, wondering whether he were worth a shot. Suddenly I felt "Blazeaway" trembling violently beneath me, and on looking over my left shoulder to discover the reason, I was startled to see two fine lions not more than a hundred yards away, evidently the pair which I had seen the day before and which we had really come in search of. They looked as if they meant to dispute our passage, for they came slowly towards me for about ten yards or so and then lay down, watching me steadily all the time. I called out to Spooner, "Here are the lions I told you about," and he whipped up the ponies and in a moment or two was beside me with the tonga.

By this time I had seized my .303 and dismounted, so we at once commenced a cautious advance on the crouching lions, the arrangement being that Spooner was to take the right-hand one and I the other. We had got to within sixty yards' range without incident and were just about to sit down comfortably to "pot" them, when they suddenly surprised us by turning and bolting off. I managed, however, to put a bullet into the one I had marked just as he crested a bank, and he looked very grand as he reared up against the sky and clawed the air on feeling the lead. For a second or two he gave me the impression that he was about to charge; but luckily he changed his mind and followed his companion, who had so far escaped scot free. I immediately mounted "Blazeaway" and galloped off in hot pursuit, and after about half a mile of very stiff going got up with them once more. Finding now that they could not get away, they halted; came to bay and then charged down upon me, the wounded lion leading. I had left my rifle behind, so all I could do was to turn and fly as fast as "Blazeaway" could go, praying inwardly the while that he would not put his foot into a hole. When the lions saw that they were unable to overtake me, they gave up the chase and lay down again, the wounded one being about two hundred yards in front of the other. At once I pulled up too, and then went back a little way, keeping a careful eye upon them; and I continued these tactics of riding up and down at a respectful distance until Spooner came up with the rifles, when we renewed the attack.

As a first measure I thought it advisable to disable the unhurt lion if possible, and, still using the .303, I got him with the second shot at a range of about three hundred yards. He seemed badly hit, for he sprang into the air and apparently fell heavily. I then exchanged my .303 for Spooner's spare 12-bore rifle, and we turned our attention to the nearer lion, who all this time had been lying perfectly still, watching our movements closely, and evidently just waiting to be down upon us the moment we came within charging distance. He was never given this opportunity, however, for we did not approach nearer than ninety yards, when Spooner sat down comfortably and knocked him over quite dead with one shot from his .577, the bullet entering the left shoulder obliquely and passing through the heart.

It was now dusk, and there was no time to be lost if we meant to bag the second lion as well. We therefore resumed our cautious advance, moving to the right, as we went, so as to get behind us what light there was remaining. The lion of course twisted round in the grass in such a way as always to keep facing us, and looked very ferocious, so that I was convinced that unless he were entirely disabled by the first shot he would be down on us like a whirlwind. All the same, I felt confident that, even in this event, one of us would succeed in stopping him before he could do any damage; but in this I was unfortunately to be proved mistaken.

Eventually we managed to get within eighty yards of the enraged animal, I being about five yards to the left front of Spooner, who was followed by Bhoota at about the same distance to his right rear. By this time the lion was beside himself with fury, growling savagely and raising quite a cloud of dust by lashing his tail against the ground. It was clearly high time that we did something, so asking Spooner to fire, dropped on one knee and waited. Nor was I kept long in suspense, for the moment Spooner's shot rang out, up jumped the lion and charged down in a bee-line for me, coming in long, low bounds at great speed. I fired the right barrel at about fifty yards, but apparently missed; the left at about half that range, still without stopping effect. I knew then that there was no time reload, so remained kneeling, expecting him to be on me the next moment. Suddenly, just as he was within a bound of me, he made a quick turn, to my right. "Good heavens," I thought, "he is going for Spooner." I was wrong in this, however, for like a flash he passed Spooner also, and with a last tremendous bound seized Bhoota by the leg and rolled over and over with him for some yards in the impetus of the rush. Finally he stood over him and tried to seize him by the throat, which the brave fellow prevented by courageously stuffing his left arm right into the great jaws. Poor Bhoota! By moving at the critical moment, he had diverted the lion's attention from me and had drawn the whole fury of the charge on to himself.

All this, of course, happened in only a second or two. In the short instant that intervened, I felt a cartridge thrust into my hand by Spooner's plucky servant, Imam Din, who had carried the 12-bore all day and who had stuck to me gallantly throughout the charge; and shoving it in, I rushed as quickly as I could to Bhoota's rescue. Meanwhile, Spooner had got there before me and when I came up actually had his left hand on the lion's flank, in a vain attempt to push him off Bhoota's prostrate body and so get at the heavy rifle which the poor fellow still stoutly clutched. The lion, however, was so busily engaged mauling Bhoota's arm that he paid not the slightest attention to Spooner's efforts. Unfortunately, as he was facing straight in my direction, I had to move up in full view of him, and the moment I reached his head, he stopped chewing the arm, though still holding it in his mouth, and threw himself back on his haunches, preparing for a spring, at the same time curling back his lips and exposing his long tusks in a savage snarl. I knew then that I had not a moment to spare, so I threw the rifle up to my shoulder and pulled the trigger. Imagine my utter despair and horror when it did not go off! "Misfire again," I thought, and my heart almost stopped beating. As took a step backwards, I felt it was all over no for he would never give me time to extract the cartridge and load again. Still I took another step backwards, keeping my eyes fixed on the lion's, which were blazing with rage; and in the middle of my third step, just as the brute was gathering himself for his spring, it suddenly struck me that in my haste and excitement, I had forgotten that I was using a borrowed rifle and had not pulled back the hammer (my own was hammerless). To do this and put a bullet through the lion's brain was then the work of a moment; and he fell dead instantly right on the top of Bhoota.

We did not lose a moment in rolling his great carcase off Bhoota's body and quickly forced opening the jaws so as to disengage the mangled arm which still remained in his mouth. By this time the poor shikari was in a fainting condition, and we flew to the tonga for the brandy flask which we had so providentially brought with us. On making a rough examination of the wounded man, we found that his left arm and right leg were both frightfully mauled, the latter being broken as well. He was lifted tenderly into the tonga -- how thankful we now were to have it with us! -- and Spooner at once set off with him to camp and the doctor.

Before following them home I made a hasty examination of the dead lion and found him to be a very good specimen in every way. I was particularly satisfied to see that one of the two shots I had fired as he charged down upon me had taken effect. The bullet had entered below the right eye, and only just missed the brain. Unfortunately it was a steel one which Spooner had unluckily brought in his ammunition bag by mistake; still one would have thought that a shot of this kind, even with a hard bullet, would at least have checked the lion for the moment. As a matter of fact, however, it went clean through him without having the slightest stopping effect. My last bullet, which was of soft lead, had entered close to the right eye and embedded itself in the brain. By this time it had grown almost dark, so I left the two dead lions where they lay and rode for camp, which I was lucky enough to reach without further adventure or mishap. I may mention here that early next morning two other lions were found devouring the one we had first shot; but they had not had time to do much damage, and the head, which I have had mounted, makes a very fine trophy indeed. The lion that mauled Bhoota was untouched.

On my arrival in camp I found that everything that was possible was being done for poor Bhoota by Dr. McCulloch, the same who had travelled up with me to Tsavo and shot the ostrich from the train on my first arrival in the country, and who was luckily on the spot. His wounds had been skilfully dressed, the broken leg put in splints, and under the influence of a soothing draught the poor fellow was soon sleeping peacefully. At first we had great hope of saving both life and limb, and certainly for some days he seemed to be getting on as well as could be expected. The wounds, however, were very bad ones, especially those on the leg where the long tusks had met through and through the flesh, leaving over a dozen deep tooth marks; the arm, though dreadfully mauled, soon healed. It was wonderful to notice how cheerfully the old shikari, bore it all, and a pleasure to listen to his tale of how he would have his revenge on the whole tribe of

97

lions as soon as he was able to get about again. But alas, his shikar was over. The leg got rapidly worse, and mortification setting in, it had to be amputated half way up the thigh.

Dr. Winston Waters performed the operation most skilfully, and curiously enough the operating table was canopied with the skin of the lion which had been responsible for the injury. Bhoota made a good recovery from the operation, but seemed to lose heart when he found that he had only one leg left, as according to his ideas he had now but a poor chance of being allowed to enter Heaven. We did all that was possible for him, and Spooner especially could not have looked after a brother more tenderly; but to our great sorrow he sank gradually, and died on July 19.

The hunt which had such a disastrous sequel proved to be the last occasion on which I met a lion in the open, as we got out of the hunting country shortly afterwards and for the rest of my stay in East Africa I had too much work to do to be able to go any distance in search of big game.

## CHAPTER XXV

### A MAN-EATER IN A RAILWAY CARRIAGE

Towards the end of my stay in British East Africa, I dined one evening with Mr. Ryall, the Superintendent of the Police, in his inspection carriage on the railway. Poor Ryall! I little thought then what a terrible fate was to overtake him only a few months later in that very carriage in which we dined.

A man-eating lion had taken up his quarters at a little roadside station called Kimaa, and had developed an extraordinary taste for the members of the railway staff. He was a most daring brute, quite indifferent as to whether he carried off the station-master, the signalman, or the pointsman; and one night, in his efforts to obtain a meal, he actually climbed up on to the roof of the station buildings and tried to tear off the corrugated-iron sheets. At this the terrified baboo in charge of the telegraph instrument below sent the following laconic message to the Traffic Manager: "Lion fighting with station. Send urgent succour." Fortunately he was not victorious in his "fight with the station"; but he tried so hard to get in that he cut his feet badly on the iron sheeting, leaving large blood-stains on the roof. Another night, however, he succeeded in carrying off the native driver of the pumping-engine, and soon afterwards added several other victims to his list. On one occasion an engine-driver arranged to sit up all night in a large iron water-tank in the hope of getting a shot at him, and had a loop-hole cut in the side of the tank from which to fire. But as so often happens, the hunter became the hunted; the lion turned up in the middle of the night, overthrew the tank and actually tried to drag the driver out through the narrow circular hole in the top through which he had squeezed in. Fortunately the tank was just too deep for the brute to be able to reach the man at the bottom; but the latter was naturally half paralysed with fear and had to crouch so low down as to be unable to take anything like proper aim. He fired, however, and succeeded in frightening the lion away for the time being.

It was in a vain attempt to destroy this pest that poor Ryall met his tragic and untimely end. On June 6, 1900, he was travelling up in his inspection carriage from Makindu to Nairobi, accompanied by two friends, Mr. Huebner and Mr. Parenti. When they reached Kimaa, which is about two hundred and fifty miles from Mombasa, they were told that the man-eater had been seen close to the station only a short time before their train arrived, so they at once made up their minds to remain there for the night and endeavour to shoot him. Ryall's carriage was accordingly detached from the train and shunted into a siding close to the station, where, owing to the unfinished state of the line, it did not stand perfectly level, but had a pronounced list to one side. In the afternoon the three friends went out to look for the lion, but, finding no traces of him whatever, they returned to the carriage for dinner. Afterwards they all sat up on guard for some time; but the only noticeable thing they saw was what they took to be two very bright and steady glow-worms. After-events proved that these could have been nothing else than the eyes of the man-eater steadily watching them all the time and studying their every movement. The hour now growing late, and there being apparently no sign of the lion, Ryall persuaded his two friends to lie down, while he kept the first watch. Huebner occupied the high berth over the table on the one side of the carriage, the only other berth being on the opposite side of the compartment and lower down. This Ryall offered to Parenti, who declined it, saying that he would be quite comfortable on the floor and he accordingly lay down to sleep, with his feet towards the sliding door which gave admission the carriage.

It is supposed that Ryall, after watching for some considerable time, must have come to the conclusion that the lion was not going to make its appearance that night, for he lay down on the lower berth and dozed off. No sooner had he done so, doubtless, than the cunning man-eater began cautiously to stalk the three sleepers. In order to reach the little platform at the end of the carriage, he had to mount two very high steps from the railway line, but these he managed to negotiate successfully and in silence. The door from this platform into the carriage was a sliding one on wheels, which ran very easily on a brass runner; and as it was probably not quite shut, or at any rate not secured in any way, it was an easy matter for the lion to thrust in a paw and shove it open. But owing to the tilt of the carriage and to his great extra weight on the one side, the door slid to and snapped into the lock the moment he got his body right in, thus leaving him shut up with the three sleeping me in the compartment.

He sprang at once at Ryall, but in order to reach him had actually to plant his feet on Parenti, who, it will be remembered, was sleeping on the floor. At this moment Huebner was suddenly awakened by a loud cry, and on looking down from his berth was horrified to see an enormous lion standing with his hind feet on Parenti's body, while his forepaws rested on poor Ryall. Small wonder that he was panic-stricken at the sight. There was only one possible way of escape, and that was through the second sliding door communicating with the servants' quarters, which was opposite to that by which the lion had entered. But in order to reach this door Huebner had literally to jump on to the man-eater's back, for its great bulk filled up all the space beneath his berth. It sounds scarcely credible, but it appears that in the excitement and horror of the moment he actually did this, and fortunately the lion was too busily engaged with his victim to pay any attention to him. So he managed to reach the door in safety; but there, to his dismay, he found that it was held fast on the other side by the terrified coolies, who had been aroused by the disturbance caused by the lion's entrance. In utter desperation he made frantic efforts to open it, and exerting all his strength at last managed to pull it back sufficiently far to allow him to squeeze through, when the trembling coolies instantly tied it up again with their turbans. A moment afterwards a great crash was heard, and the whole carriage lurched violently to one side; the lion had broken through one of the windows, carrying off poor Ryall with him. Being now released, Parenti lost no time in jumping through the window on the opposite side of the carriage, and fled for refuge to one of the station buildings; his escape was little short of miraculous, as the lion had been actually standing on him as he lay on the floor. The carriage itself was badly shattered, and the wood-work of the window had been broken to pieces by the passage of the lion as he sprang through with his victim in his mouth.

All that can be hoped is that poor Ryall's death was instantaneous. His remains were found next morning about a quarter of a mile away in the bush, and were taken to Nairobi for burial. I am glad to be able to add that very shortly afterwards the terrible brute who was responsible for this awful tragedy was caught in an ingenious trap constructed by one of the railway staff. He was kept on view for several days, and then shot.

# CHAPTER XXVI

## WORK AT NAIROBI

Although the lion which caused poor Bhoota's death was the last I managed to shoot in East Africa, I saw several others afterwards while travelling up and down the line at different times on construction work. In particular, I remember one very curious incident which happened early on the morning of June 2, when I was travelling towards Nairobi, accompanied by Dr. McCulloch. The Doctor was going home on leave in the course of a few days, and was bemoaning to me his bad luck in never having shot or even seen a lion all the time he had been in the country. We were standing on the engine at the time, facing each other, he with his back to the north.

"My dear Mac," I said, "it is because you don't look out for them."

"Rubbish," he retorted; "I do nothing else when I am out hunting."

"Well," I replied, "are you really very anxious to shoot one before you go home?"

"I would rather get a lion than anything else in the world," was the emphatic reply.

"Very good, then. Sultan," I called to the driver, "stop the engine."

"Now, Mac," I continued, as the train was quickly brought to a standstill, "here's a chance for you. Just jump off and bag those two over there."

He turned round in blank astonishment and could hardly believe his eyes when he saw two fine lions only about two hundred yards off, busily engaged in devouring a wildebeeste which they had evidently just killed. I had spotted them almost as soon as Mac had begun to talk of his bad luck, and had only waited to tell him until we got nearer, so as to give him a greater surprise. He was off the engine in a second and made directly for the two beasts. Just as he was about to fire one of them bolted, so I called out to him to shoot the other quickly before he too made good his escape. This one was looking at us over his shoulder with one paw on the dead wildebeeste, and while he stood in this attitude Mac dropped him with a bullet through the heart. Needless to say he was tremendously delighted with his success, and after the dead lion had been carried to the train and propped up against a carriage, I took a photograph of him standing beside his fine trophy.

Three days after this incident railhead reached Nairobi, and I was given charge of the new division of the line. Nairobi was to be the headquarters of the Railway

101

Administration, so there was an immense amount of work to be done in converting an absolutely bare plain, three hundred and twenty-seven miles from the nearest place where even a nail could be purchased, into a busy railway centre. Roads and bridges had to be constructed, houses and work-shops built, turntables and station quarters erected, a water supply laid on, and a hundred and one other things done which go to the making of a railway township. Wonderfully soon, however, the nucleus of the present town began to take shape, and a thriving "bazaar" sprang into existence with a mushroom-like growth. In this, however, a case or two of plague broke out before very long, so I gave the natives and Indians who inhabited it an hour's notice to clear out, and on my own responsibility promptly burned the whole place to the ground. For this somewhat arbitrary proceeding I was mildly called over the coals, as I expected; but all the same it effectually stamped out the plague, which did not reappear during the time I was in the country.

With a little persuasion I managed to induce several hundred of the Wa Kikuyu, in whose country we now were, to come and work at Nairobi, and very useful and capable they proved themselves after a little training. They frequently brought me in word that the shambas (plantations, gardens) at the back of the hill on which my camp was pitched were being destroyed by elephants, but unfortunately I could never spare time to go out in quest of them. On one occasion, however, I passed the news on to my friend, Dr. Winston Waters, with the result that he had a most exciting adventure with a big bull elephant. He set out in quest of the depredator, and, guided by a few of the Wa Kikuyu, soon came upon him hidden among some shady trees. Waters was a great believer in a close shot, so he stalked up to within a few yards of the animal and then fired his .577, aiming for the heart. The elephant responded by a prompt and determined charge, and although Waters quickly let him have the left barrel as well, it proved of no effect; and on he came, screaming and trumpeting with rage. There was nothing for it, therefore, but to fly for dear life; so down a path raced Waters for all he was worth, the elephant giving vigorous chase and gaining rapidly. In a few seconds matters began to look very serious for the sportsman, for the huge monster was almost on him; but at the critical moment he stepped on to the false cover of a carefully-concealed game pit and disappeared from view as if by magic. This sudden descent of his enemy apparently into the bowels of the earth so startled the elephant that he stopped short in his career and made off into the jungle. As for Waters, he was luckily none the worse for his fall, as the pit was neither staked at the bottom nor very deep; he soon scrambled out, and, following up the wounded elephant, succeeded in finishing him off without further trouble.

Towards the end of 1899 I left for England. A few days before I started all my Wa Kikuyu "children", as they called themselves, came in a body and begged to be taken with me. I pictured to them the cold, wet climate of England and its great distance from their native land; but they assured me that these were nothing to them, as they only wished to continue my "children" and to go wherever I went. I could hardly imagine myself arriving in London with a body-guard of four hundred more or less naked savages, but it was only with difficulty that I persuaded them that they had better remain in their own country. The ever-faithful Mahina, my "boy" Roshan Khan, my honest chaukidar, Meeanh, and a few other coolies who had been a long time with me, accompanied me to the coast, where they bade me a sorrowful farewell and left for India the day before I sailed on my homeward journey.

# CHAPTER XXVII

## THE FINDING OF THE NEW ELAND

During the early part of last year (1906) I revisited the scene of my former labours and adventures on a shooting trip. Unfortunately the train by which I travelled up from Mombasa reached Tsavo at midnight, but all the same I got out and prowled about as long as time would permit, half wondering every moment if the ghosts of the two man-eaters would spring at me out of the bushes. I wanted very much to spend a day or two in the old place, but my companions were anxious to push on as quickly as possible to better hunting-grounds. I took the trouble, however, to wake them out of their peaceful slumbers in order to point out to them, by the pale moonlight, the strength and beauty of the Tsavo bridge; but I fear this delicate little attention was scarcely appreciated as it deserved. Naturally I could not expect them, or anyone else, to view the bridge quite from my point of view; I looked on it as a child of mine, brought up through stress and danger and troubles of all kinds, but the ordinary traveller of course knows nothing of this and doubtless thinks it only a very commonplace and insignificant structure indeed.

We spent a few days at Nairobi, now a flourishing town of some 6,000 inhabitants, supplied with every modern comfort and luxury, including a well laid-out race course; and after a short trip to Lake Victoria Nyanza and Uganda, we made our way back to the Eldama Ravine, which lies some twenty miles north of Landiani Station in the province of Naivasha. Here we started in earnest on our big game expedition, which I am glad to say proved to be a most delightful and interesting one in every way. The country was lovely, and the climate cool and bracing. We all got a fair amount of sport, our bag including rhino, hippo, waterbuck, reedbuck, hartebeeste, wildebeeste, ostrich, impala, oryx, roan antelope, etc.; but for the present I must confine myself to a short account of how I was lucky enough to shoot a specimen of an entirely new race of eland.

Our party of five, including one lady who rode and shot equally straight, left the Eldama Ravine on January 22, and trekked off in an easterly direction across the Laikipia Plateau. As the trail which we were to take was very little known and almost impossible

103

to follow without a guide, Mr. Foaker, the District Officer at the Ravine, very kindly procured us a reliable man -- a young Uashin Gishu Masai named Uliagurma. But as he could not speak a word of Swahili, we had also to engage an interpreter, an excellent, cheery fellow of the same tribe named Landaalu; and he in his turn possessed a kinsman who insisted on coming too, although he was no earthly use to us. Our route took us through the Solai Swamp, over the Multilo and Subu Ko Lultian ranges, and across many unexpected rivers and streamlets. On our first march I noticed that Uliagurma, our kirongozi (guide), was suffering extremely, though uncomplainingly, from earache, so I told him to come to me when we got to camp and I would see what I could do for him. Strange to say, my doctoring proved most successful, and Uliagurma was so grateful that he spread my fame as a "medicine-man" far and wide among the natives wherever we trekked. The consequence was that men, women and children in every state of disease and crippledom came and besieged our camps, begging for some of the magical dawa (medicine). I used to do what I could, and only hope I did not injure many of them; but it was heartrending to see some of the quite hopeless cases I was expected to cure.

After we had climbed the Subu Ko Lultian and got a footing on the plateau, we pitched our camp on the banks of the Angarua river, where we found a big Masai kraal, the inhabitants of which seemed much astonished at our sudden appearance in their neighbourhood. They were very friendly, however, and visited our camp in swarms an hour or so after our arrival. Riding my pony and accompanied by Landaalu as interpreter, and my gun-bearer Juma, I returned their call in the afternoon, when the elmorani (warriors) gave for my entertainment an exhibition of the gymnastic exercises which they practise regularly in order more particularly to strengthen their legs and render them supple. After the performance I asked if there was any game about and was told that some might be found a few miles to the north of the kraal; so I set out at once with Landaalu and Juma to try my luck. It was a perfect afternoon, and no sooner had I cleared the belt of scrub which grew round the kraal, when by the aid of my glasses I saw a herd of zebra and other game away in the distance, feeding peacefully on the rolling prairie. I made my way steadily towards them, and noticed as I went that a couple of eland were gradually drawing away from the rest of the herd. I marked these for my own, and carefully noting the direction they were taking, I dismounted and made a detour round a rise so as to lie in wait for them and cut them off. My plan succeeded admirably, for the two fine animals continued to come straight towards me without suspicion, feeding quietly by the way. When they got to within eighty yards or so, I picked out the bigger head and was only waiting for him to make a slight turn before pulling the trigger, when bang went the heavy rifle of one of my companions about half a mile away. In an instant the two eland had bounded off, and I decided not to risk a shot, in the hope that they would soon settle down again and give me another chance.

Mentally blessing my friend for firing at this untimely moment, I watched them make for a belt of wood about a mile further on, hoping against hope that they would remain on the near side of it. No such luck, however, for they plunged into it and were quickly swallowed up out of my sight. Running to my pony, which Landaalu had dexterously brought up, I galloped in the direction of the spot in the trees where the eland had disappeared; but imagine my vexation when I found that I had to pull up sharp on the edge of a nasty-looking swamp, which at first sight appeared too boggy and treacherous to attempt to cross. I rode up and down it without being able to find anything like a really safe crossing place, so in desperation I at last determined to take the risk of crossing it along an old rhino path where the reeds were flattened down. My pony floundered bravely through, and eventually succeeded in getting safely to the other side. I then made my way cautiously through the belt of trees, and was relieved to find that it was only half a mile or so broad. I dismounted as I neared the further side, and, tying my pony to a tree, crept quietly forward, expecting to see the eland not far off; but to my disappointment there was no trace of game of any kind on the whole wide stretch of country that met my view. I therefore tried another direction, and, taking a half turn to my left, made my way carefully through some open glades to the top of a little rise not far off.

The sight that now met my eyes fairly took my breath away; for there, not three hundred yards off and stalking placidly along at a slow walk, was a herd of fully a hundred eland of all ages and sizes. The rear of the column was brought up by a magnificent old bull, and my heart jumped for joy as I watched him from the shelter of the bushes behind which I lay concealed. The next thing to be done was to decide on a plan of attack, and this had to be thought of without loss of time, for the wind was blowing from me almost in the direction of the eland, who would certainly scent me very soon if I did not get away. Quickly noting the direction in which they were moving, I saw that if all went well they ought to pass close to a little hillock about a mile or so off; and if I were very sharp about it, I thought I could make a circuit through the wood and be on this rise, in a good position for both wind and cover, before the herd could reach it. Accordingly I crept away with the object of finding my mount, but to my delight -- just behind me and well hidden -- stood the undefeated Landaalu, who in some mysterious way had followed me up, found the pony where I had left it tied to a tree, and brought it on to me. With a bright grin on his face he thrust the reins into my hand, and I was up and galloping off in an instant.

I soon discovered that I had further to go than I expected, for I was forced to make a big detour in order to keep out of sight of the herd; but on halting once or twice and peeping through the trees I saw that all was going well and that they were still calmly moving on in the right direction. The last quarter of a mile had to be negotiated in the open, but I found that by lying flat down on my pony's back I was completely hidden from the advancing herd by an intervening swell in the ground. In this manner I managed to get unobserved to the lee of my hillock, where I dismounted, threw the reins over a stump, and crawled stealthily but as quickly as I could to the top. I was in great doubt as to whether I should be in time or not, but on peering, hatless, over the crest, I was overjoyed to find the whole herd just below me. One of the eland, not twenty yards off, saw me at once, and stood still to gaze at me in astonishment. It was a female, however, so I took no notice of her, but looked round to see if my great bull were anywhere near. Yes, there he was; he had passed the spot where I lay, but was not more than forty yards off, moving in the same leisurely fashion as when I first saw him. An instant later, he noticed the general alarm caused by my appearance, and stopped and turned half round to see what was the matter. This gave me my opportunity, so I fired, aiming behind the shoulder. The way in which he jumped and kicked on feeling the lead told me I had hit him hard, and I got two more bullets into him from the magazine of my .303 before he managed to gain the shelter of a neighbouring thicket and was lost to sight. In the meantime the whole herd had thundered off at full gallop, disappearing in a few minutes in a cloud of dust.

I was confident that there would be little difficulty in finding the wounded eland, and on Landaalu coming up -- which, by the way, he did almost immediately, for he was a wonderful goer -- we started to make a rough search through the thicket. Owing to the growing darkness, however, we met with no success, so I decided to return to camp, which was many miles away, and to resume the quest at daybreak the following morning. It turned out that we were even further from home than I thought, and black night came upon us before we had covered a quarter of the distance. Fortunately the invaluable Landaalu had discovered a good crossing over the swamp, so we were able to press on at a good pace without losing any time in overcoming the obstacle. After an hour or so of hard travelling, we were delighted to see a rocket go up, fired by my friends to guide us on our way. Such a sight is wonderfully cheering when one is far away from camp, trudging along in the inky darkness and none too certain of one's direction; and a rocket equipment should invariably be carried by the traveller in the wilds. Several more were sent up before we got anywhere near camp, and I remarked to Landaalu that we must have gone a very long way after the eland. "Long way," he replied; "why, Master, we have been to Baringo!" This lake as a matter of fact was fully fifty miles away. When finally we arrived I fired the ardour of my companions by relating the adventures of the afternoon and telling them of the wonderful herd I had seen; and it was at once agreed that we should stay where we were for a day or two in the hope of good sport being obtained.

As soon as it was daylight the next morning I sent out a party of our porters with full instructions where to find my eland, which I was sure must be lying somewhere in the thicket close to the hill from where I had shot him; and very shortly afterwards we ourselves made a start. After a couple of hours' travelling we were lucky enough to catch sight of a portion of the herd of eland, when we dismounted and stalked them carefully through the long grass. All of a sudden one popped up its head unexpectedly about fifty yards away. One of my companions immediately levelled his rifle at it, but from where I was I could see better than he that the head was a poor one, and so called out to him not to fire. The warning came too late, however, for at that moment he pulled the trigger. It was rather a difficult shot, too, as the body of the animal could not be seen very well owing to the height of the grass; still, as the head instantly disappeared we hoped for the best and ran up to the place, but no trace of the eland could be found. Accordingly we pushed on again and after a little rested for a short time under the shade of some trees. We had gone about three miles after resuming our search for game, when one of the porters remembered that he had left the water-bottle he was carrying at the trees where we had halted, so he was sent back for it with strict injunctions to make haste and to rejoin us as quickly as possible. Curiously enough, this trifling incident proved quite providential; for the porter (whose name was Sabaki), after recovering the water-bottle, found himself unable to trace us through the jungle and accordingly struck home for camp. On his way back he actually stumbled over the dead body of the eland which I had shot the previous day and which the search party I had sent out in the morning had failed to find. They were still looking for it close at hand, however, so Sabaki hailed them and they at once set to work to skin and cut up the animal, and then carried it to the camp.

Meanwhile, of course, we knew nothing of all this, and continued our hunt for game. Shortly after noon we had a light lunch, and while we were eating it our guides, Uliagurma and Landaalu, discovered a bees' nest in a fallen tree and proceeded to try to extract the honey, of which the Masai are very fond. This interference was naturally strongly resented by the bees, and soon the semi-naked youths ran flying past us with the angry swarm in full pursuit. I laughed heartily at Landaalu, and chaffed him unmercifully for allowing himself, a Masai, to be put to flight by a few bees. This the jolly fellow took very good-humouredly, saying that if he only had a jacket like mine he would soon go and get the honey. I gave him my jacket at once, and a most comical figure he cut in it, as it was very short and he had practically nothing else on. When the nest was properly examined, however, it was found that the bees had eaten all the honey; so after taking some photographs of our guides at work among the bees we all proceeded homewards, reaching camp about dusk, with nothing to show for our long day's hunt.

We were met by Sabaki, who was in a great state of excitement, and who started to explain in very bad Swahili how he had come across the dead eland. Misunderstanding what he said, I told my friend that Sabaki had found the eland which he had shot in the morning, and rejoiced heartily with him at this piece of good luck. On viewing the head, however, we could not understand it, as it was very much bigger than the one he had fired at; and it was not till later in the evening when I visited Landaalu, curled up at the camp fire, that the mystery was explained. He greeted me by saying that after all we had not gone to Baringo for nothing the previous day, and on my asking him what he meant he told me about the finding of the eland, taking it for granted that I knew it was mine. I quickly called up Sabaki and after some trouble got from him the whole story of how he had found the body close to my little hillock and near where my men were searching for it. So I broke the truth gently to my friend, who at once acknowledged my claim and congratulated me on my good fortune.

How great this good fortune was I did not know till long after; but even then, when I came to examine the head and skin carefully, I found that they both differed materially from those of any other eland that I had ever seen. For one thing, there was no long tuft of hair on the forehead, while from the lower corner of each eye ran an incomplete white stripe similar to, though smaller than, those found in the giant eland. The sides of the forehead were of a reddish colour, and on the lower part of the face there was a much larger brown patch than is to be seen on the ordinary eland. The striping on the body was very slight, the chief markings being three lines across the withers. On my return to England in April. I sent the head to Rowland Ward's to be set up, and while there it was seen by Mr. R. Lydekker, F.R.S., of the British Museum, the well-known naturalist and specialist in big game, who wrote to tell me that it possessed great zoological interest, as showing the existence of a hitherto unknown race of eland. Mr.

Lydekker also contributed the following notice describing the animal to The Field of September 29, 1906:

"Considerable interest attaches to the head of an eland, killed by Colonel J.H. Patterson in British East Africa, and set up by Mr. Rowland Ward, on account of certain peculiarities in colouring and markings, which indicate a transition from the ordinary South African animal in the direction of the giant eland (Taurotragus derbianus) of the Bahr-el-Ghazal district and West Africa. In the striped variety (Taurotragus oryx livingstonianus) of the ordinary South African eland, the whole middle line of the face of the adult bull is uniformly dark, or even blackish-brown, with a tuft of long bushy hair on the forehead, and no white stripe from the lower angle of the eye. On the other hand, in the Sudani form of the giant eland (T. derbianus gigas), as represented by a bull figured by Mr. Rothschild in Novitates Zoologicae for 1905, the upper part of the face has the hair rufous and shorter than in the ordinary eland, while from the lower angle of each eye a white stripe runs inwards and downwards, recalling the white chevron of the kudu, although the two stripes do not meet in the middle line.

"In Colonel Patterson's eland (which may well be designated T. oryx pattersonianus) there is an incomplete white chevron similar to, although rather smaller than, the one found in the giant eland, while only a narrow stripe in the middle line of the face, above and between the eyes, is dark-brown, the sides of the forehead being rufous. On the lower part of the face there is a larger dark-brown area than in the ordinary eland, although there is a rufous fawn-coloured patch on each side above the nostril. In both the latter respects Colonel Patterson's specimen recalls the giant eland, although it apparently lacks the dark white-bordered band on the side of the neck, characteristic of the latter. If all the elands from that part of Portuguese East Africa where Colonel Patterson's specimen was obtained turn out to be of the same type, there will be a strong presumption that the true and the giant eland, like the various local forms of giraffe and bonte-quagga, are only races of one and the same species. While, even if the present specimen be only a 'sport' (which I consider unlikely), it will serve to show that the southern and northern elands are more nearly related than has hitherto been supposed."

As my eland thus proved to be of some considerable scientific value, and as the authorities of the British Museum expressed a desire to possess its head, I gladly presented it to the Trustees, so that all sportsmen and naturalists might have an opportunity of seeing it at the Natural History Museum at South Kensington, where it now is.

# APPENDIX

## I.

SPORTSMEN who think of visiting British East Africa on a shooting trip may be glad of a few general hints on points of interest and importance.

The battery, to be sufficient for all needs, should consist of a .450 express, a .303 sporting rifle, and a 12-bore shot gun; and I should consider 250 rounds of .450 (50 hard and 200 soft), 300 rounds of .303 (100 hard and 200 soft), and 500 12-bore shot cartridges of say, the 6 and 8 sizes, sufficient for a three months' trip. Leather bandoliers to carry 50 each of these different cartridges would also prove very useful.

A couple of hundred rockets of various colours should certainly be taken, as they are invaluable for signalling to and from camp after dark. These can be obtained so as to fire from a 12-bore shot gun or from a short pistol, and some should always be left with the camp neopara (Headman) for use as occasion requires.

The rifles, cartridges, and rockets should be consigned to an agent in Mombasa, and sent off from London in tin-lined cases at least a month before the sportsman himself intends to start. It must be remembered that the Customs House at Mombasa charges a 10 per cent duty on the value of all articles imported, so that the invoices should be preserved and produced for inspection.

The hunter's kit should include a good pith sunhat, a couple of suits of khaki, leather gaiters or a couple of pairs of puttees, wash-leather gloves to protect the hands from the sun, and two pairs of boots with hemp soles; long Norwegian boots will also be found very useful. The usual underclothing worn in England is all that is required if the shooting is to be done in the highlands. A good warm overcoat will be much appreciated up-country in the cool of the evenings, and a light mackintosh for wet weather ought also to be included. For use in rocky or thorny country, a pair of knee and elbow pads will be found invaluable, and those who feel the sun should also provide themselves with a spine-protector. The latter is a most useful article of kit, for although the air may be pretty cool, the sun strikes down very fiercely towards midday. A well-filled medicine chest should of course not be forgotten.

A good field glass, a hunting and skinning knife or two, and a Kodak with about 200 films should also be carried. With regard to the last item, I should strongly advise all who intend to take photographs on their trip to pay a visit to Mr. W.D. Young on arriving at Nairobi. He is an enthusiastic photographer, and will gladly give advice to all as to light and time of exposure; and as these are the two points which require most attention, hints from some one of experience in the country are most useful. I myself am much indebted to Mr. Young's kindly advice, and I am sure I should not have achieved much success in my pictures without it. I made it a practice on my last visit to the country to send him the exposed films for development whenever I reached a postal station, and I should recommend others to do the same, as films deteriorate rapidly on the voyage home; indeed I had nearly four hundred spoiled in this way, taken when I was in the country in 1898-99.

As regards camp equipment, all that need be taken out from England are a small double-fly tent, three Jaeger blankets, a collapsible bath, a Wolseley valise, and a good filter; and even these can be obtained just as good locally. Chop boxes (food) and other necessary camp gear should be obtained at Mombasa or Nairobi, where the agents will put up just what is necessary. About a month before sailing from England a letter should be sent to the agents, stating the date of arrival and what porters, etc., will be required. The sportsman will then find everything ready for him, so that an immediate start may be made.

Unless money is no object, I should not advise anyone to engage porters at Mombasa, as equally good men can be obtained at Nairobi, thus saving 20 rupees per head in return railway fares. It must be remembered that for transport work men are infinitely preferable to donkeys, as the latter are exasperatingly slow and troublesome, especially on rough ground or on crossing streams, where every load has to be unpacked, carried over, and then reloaded on the animal's back. The caravan for one sportsman -- if he intends going far from the railway -- is usually made up as follows, though the exact numbers depend upon many considerations:

1 Headman ............... 50 rupees[1] per month.

1 Cook ............... 35 "

1 Gun-bearer ............... 20 "

1 "Boy" (personal servant) ............... 20 "

2 Askaris (armed porters) ............... 12 " " each.

30 Porters ............... 10 " " each.

[1] The rupee in British East Africa is on the basis of 15 to the pound sterling.

The porters are all registered, the Government taking a small fee for the registration; and according to custom half the wages due for the whole trip are advanced to the men before a start is made. The sportsman is obliged to provide each porter with a jersey, blanket and water-bottle, while the gun-bearer and "boy" get a pair of boots in addition. A cotton shelter-tent and a cooking pot must also be furnished for every five men.

The food for the caravan is mostly rice, of which the Headman gets two kibabas (a kibaba is about 1-1/2 lb.) per day; the cook, gun-bearer, "boy" and askaris one and a half kibabas, and the ordinary porters, one kibaba, each per day.

It is the duty of the Headman to keep discipline on the safari (caravan journey), both in camp and on the march, and to see to the distribution and safety of the loads, the pitching and striking of camp, the issue of posho (food) to the porters, etc. He always brings up the rear of the caravan, and on him depends greatly the general comfort of the sportsman. For our trip at the beginning of 1906, we managed to secure a splendid neapara, and never had the least trouble with the porters all the time. His only drawback was that he could not speak English, but he told me when he left us that he was going to learn. Anybody securing him as Headman will be lucky; his name is Munyaki bin Dewani, and he can easily be found at Mombasa.

The cook is also an important member of the caravan, and a good one should be procured if possible. It is wonderful what an experienced native mpishi (cook) can turn out in the way of a meal in a few minutes after camp is pitched.

As gun-bearer, most hunters prefer a Somali. I have never tried one, but am told that they are inclined to be troublesome; they certainly rate themselves very highly, and demand about four times as much wages as an equally good Swahili.

In camp, the duties of the askaris are to keep up the fire and watch at night, and to pitch and strike the Bwana's (Master's) tent. On the march one leads the caravan, the other brings up the rear; they give assistance in the event of any trouble with the loads, see that no desertions take place, allow no straggling and generally do what they can to protect the caravan. They are each armed with an old snider rifle and 10 rounds of ball cartridge, and are generally very dangerous men to their friends when they take it into their heads to fire their weapons.

The ordinary porters will carry their 60-lb. loads day in and day out without complaint, so long as they are well fed; but stint them of their rice, and they at once become sulky mutineers. In addition to carrying the loads, they pitch and strike camp, procure firewood and water, and build grass huts if a stay of more than a day is intended to be made at one place. On the whole, the Swahili porter is one of the jolliest and most willing fellows in the world, and I have nothing but praise for him.

It may be that our sportsman intends to confine his shooting trip to the neighbourhood of the railway; in this case, the best plan is to hire one of the special carriages from the Traffic Manager of the Uganda Railway. These carriages, which have good sleeping, cooking, and bath accommodation, can be attached to almost any train, and moved from station to station or left standing in a siding at the directions of the hunter. This is the cheapest and most comfortable way of spending a short time in the country, as no tent, camp equipment, or regular porters are required; and some quite good sport can be obtained into the bargain.

Again, if the hunter intends shooting, say, in the Kenya Province, as many porters as he requires may be obtained from the official in charge at Fort Hall. The pay of the Kikuyu porter in such circumstances is only two annas a day, while he provides his own food; neither is the sportsman asked to furnish him with a blanket, jersey, and water-bottle so long as he is not taken out of his own Province. Each Province is, in fact, governed as regards porters by its own special conditions, which can easily be ascertained on arrival in the country.

There are three lines of steamers which have direct sailings to Mombasa about once a month. Two of these (the Union-Castle and the German East African Lines) sail from Southampton, calling at Marseilles, while the third (the Messageries-Maritimes) starts from the latter port. As a rule travellers to East Africa journey by the overland route to Marseilles and thence on by steamer to Mombasa -- the whole journey from London averaging about eighteen days.

The present fares for the best accommodation from London to Mombasa by the Union-Castle Line (including railway ticket to Marseilles) are as follows First-Class Single, about 48 pounds; Return (available for one year) about 93 pounds.

The fares by the German East African Line (including railway ticket to Marseilles) are:-- First-Class; Single, about 48 pounds. The Return fare (available for one; year) is double the Single fare, less 10 per cent, of ocean part of journey.

By the Messageries-Maritimes Line the through First-Class Single fare from London to Mombasa (including railway ticket to Marseilles) is about 48 pounds. The Return fare (available for two years) is about 72 pounds.

Fairly good hotel accommodation can be had at both Mombasa and Nairobi.

Before any shooting can be done it is necessary to take out a Game License, which may be obtained without difficulty at either of these two centres. This license (which costs 50 pounds) imposes an obligation on the sportsman to make a return before he leaves the country of every animal shot by him. By obtaining a special license two elephants, a giraffe, greater kudu, buffalo and eland may be shot; but there are various stipulations and fees attaching to this license which alter from time to time.

Fairly good maps of the country may be obtained at Stanford's, Long Acre, W.C., while the Game Laws and Regulations can be procured from the Colonial Office in Downing Street.

Passenger trains leave Mombasa at 11 a.m. on Mondays, Wednesdays, Fridays, and Saturdays, and are timed to arrive at Nairobi at 11:15 next morning and at Kisumu (the railway terminus on Lake Victoria Nyanza) at 9 o'clock on the morning following. The First-Class Return fares from Mombasa to Nairobi, Kisumu, and Entebbe are 5 pounds 17s. 9d., 10 pounds 10s. 3d., and 13 pounds 13s. 3d. respectively.

It is unnecessary to specify district by district when particular species of game are to be found, for the sportsman can easily learn this for himself and get the latest news of game movements on his arrival at Mombasa. As a matter of fact, the whole country abounds in game, and there cannot be lack of sport and trophies for the keen shikari. The heads and skins should be very carefully sun-dried and packed in tin-lined cases with plenty of moth-killer for shipment home. For mounting his trophies the sportsman cannot do better, I think, than go to Rowland Ward of Piccadilly. I have had mine set up by this firm for years past, and have always found their work excellent.

I consider that 400 pounds should cover the entire cost of a three months' shooting trip to East Africa, including passage both ways. The frugal sportsman will doubtless do it on less, while the extravagant man will probably spend very much more.

Should time be available, a trip to the Victoria Nyanza should certainly be made. The voyage round the Lake in one of the comfortable railway steamers takes about eight days, but the crossing to Entebbe, the official capital of Uganda, can be done in seventeen hours, though it usually takes twenty-seven, as at night the boats anchor for shelter under the lee of an island. The steamer remains long enough in Entebbe harbour to enable the energetic traveller to pay a flying visit in a rickshaw to Kampala, the native capital, some twenty-one miles off. I spent a most interesting day last year in this way, and had a chat with the boy King of Uganda, Daudi Chwa, at Mengo. He was then about nine years old, and very bright and intelligent. He made no objection to my taking his photograph, but it unfortunately turned out a failure.

It is curious to find the Baganda (i.e., people of Uganda) highly civilised -- the majority are Christians -- surrounded as they are on all sides by nations of practically naked savages; and it is a very interesting, sight to watch them in the "bazaar" at Kampala, clad in long flowing cotton garments, and busily engaged in bartering the products of the country under the shade of tattered umbrellas. Unfortunately the great scourge of the district round the shores of the Lake is the sleeping sickness, which in the past few years has carried off thousands of the natives, and has quite depopulated the islands, which were once densely inhabited. The disease is communicated by the bite of an infected fly, but happily this pest is only found in certain well-defined regions, so that if the traveller avoids these he is quite as safe, as regards sleeping sickness, as if he had remained in England.

113

On the return journey from Entebbe, Jinja, a port on the north side of the Victoria Nyanza, is usually called at. This place is of great interest, as it is here that the Lake narrows into a breadth of only a few hundred yards, and, rushing over the Ripon Falls, forms the long-sought-for source of the Nile. The magnificent view of the mighty river stretching away to the north amid enchanting scenery is most inspiring and one can well imagine how elated Speke must have felt when after enduring countless hardships, he at last looked upon it and thus solved one of the great problems the ancients.

II.

The following, is a literal translation of the Hindustani poem referred to in Chapter IX:--

IN THE NAME OF ALLAH, THE MERCIFUL, THE COMPASSIONATE:

First must I speak to the praise and glory of God, who is infinite and incomprehensible,

Who is without fault or error, who is the Life, though without body or breath.

He has no relatives, nor father nor son, being himself incomparable and passionless.

His is the knowledge of the known and of the unknown, and although without a tongue,
yet does he speak in mighty tones.

I, Roshan, came to this country of Africa, and did find it indeed a strange land;

Many rocks, mountains, and dense forests abounding in lions and leopards;

Also buffaloes, wolves, deer, rhinoceroses, elephants, camels, and all enemies of man;

Gorillas, ferocious monkeys that attack men, black baboons of giant size, spirits, and
thousands of varieties of birds;

Wild horses, wild dogs, black snakes, and all animals that a hunter or sportsman could desire.

The forests are so dark and dreadful that even the boldest warriors shrink from their awful depths.

Now from the town of Mombasa, a railway line extends unto Uganda;

In the forests bordering on this line, there are found those lions called "man-eaters," and moreover these forests are full of thorns and prickly shrubs.

Portions of this railway from Mombasa to Uganda are still being made, and here these lions fell on the workmen and destroyed them.

Such was their habit, day and night, and hundreds of men fell victims to these savage creatures, whose very jaws were steeped in blood.

Bones, flesh, skin and blood, they devoured all, and left not a trace behind them.

Because of the fear of these demons some seven or eight hundred of the labourers deserted, and remained idle;

Some two or three hundred still remained, but they were haunted by this terrible dread,

And because of fear for their lives, would sit in their huts, their hearts full of foreboding and terror.

Every one of them kept a fire burning at night, and none dared to close his eyes in sleep; yet would some of them be carried away to destruction.

The lion's roar was such that the very earth would tremble at the sound, and where was the man who did not feel afraid?

On all sides arose weeping and wailing, and the people would sit and cry like cranes, complaining of the deeds of the lions.

I, Roshan, chief of my people, also complained and prayed to God, the Prophet, and to our spiritual adviser.

And now will I relate the story of the Engineer in charge of the line.

He kept some ten or twenty goats, for the sake of their milk;

But one night a wild beast came, and destroyed them all, not one being left.

And in the morning it was reported by the watchman, who also stated that the man-eater was daily destroying the labourers and workmen, and doing great injury;

And they took the Engineer with them and showed him the footprints of the animal.

And after seeing what the animal had done, the Englishman spoke, and said,

"For this damage the lion shall pay his life." And when night came he took his gun and in very truth destroyed the beast.

Patterson Sahib is indeed a brave and valiant man, like unto those Persian heroes of old -- Rustem, Zal, Sohrab and Berzoor;

So brave is he, that the greatest warriors stood aghast at his action;

Tall in stature, young, most brave and of great strength is he.

From the other side of the line came the noise and cries of those who complained that these savage beasts were eating and destroying men,

For such has been the habit of lions from time immemorial, and groups of people have fallen victims to their fury.

Those who were proud or boastful, have but sacrificed their lives uselessly;

But to-day Patterson Sahib will watch for the lion himself!

For the people have complained loudly, and the valiant one has gone forth with his gun into the forest.

Soon after the people had retired at night to their tents, the fearless lion made his appearance;

Patterson Sahib loaded both barrels of his gun and went forth against him.

He fired many times in succession and totally paralysed the animal.

116

The lion roared like thunder as the bullets found their way to his heart.

This Englishman, Patterson, is most brave, and is indeed the very essence of valour;

Lions do not fear lions, yet one glance from Patterson Sahib cowed the bravest of them.

He fled, making for the forest, while the bullets followed hard after him;

So was this man-eater rendered helpless; he lay down in despair,

And after he had covered a chain's distance, the savage beast fell down, a corpse.

Now the people, bearing lights in their hands, all ran to look at their dead enemy.

But the Sahib said "Return, my children; the night is dark, do not rush into danger."

And in the morning all the people saw the lion lying dead.

And then the Sahib said, "Do not think of work to-day -- make holiday, enjoy and be merry."

So the people had holiday and made merry with friends from whom they had been long parted, on account of the lion:

And the absence of those who had run away was forgiven, and their money allowed them -- A generous action, comparable to the forgiveness of God and the Prophet to sinners and criminals on the day of judgment.

Oh! poet, leave this kind of simile, it is too deep for thee;

We mortals have the Devil, like unto a fierce lion, ever after us;

Oh! Roshan, may God, the Prophet, and your spiritual adviser, safeguard you day and night!

One lion, however, remained, and for fear of him all went in dread;

Sixteen days passed, all being well, and everyone enjoyed a peaceful mind;

117

But again, on the seventeenth day, the lion appeared and remained from sunset to sunrise.

He kept on roaming about in the neighbourhood like a general reconnoitring the enemy's position.

On the following day the Sahib sent for the people and warned them all to be careful of their lives;

"Do not go out from the afternoon even until the following morning," he said.

Now this was the night of Shab-i-Kadr, a Muslim festival:

And at night when all had retired to rest, the lion came in a rage,

And Patterson Sahib went forth into the field to meet him.

And when he saw the beast, he fired quickly, bullet after bullet.

The lion made a great uproar, and fled for his life, but the bullets nevertheless found a resting-place in his heart.

And everyone began to shriek and groan in their uneasy sleep, jumping up in fear, when unexpectedly the roaring of the lion was heard.

All thought of sleep was banished, and fear came in its place:

And the Sahib gave emphatic orders that no one should go out, or roam about.

And in the morning we followed the marks of blood that had flowed from the wounded animal,

And some five or seven chains away, we found the lion, lying wounded and in great pain.

And when the Sahib saw the animal he fired bullets incessantly;

But when the lion saw the Sahib, the savage animal, burning with rage, and pain,

Came by leaps and bounds close to the Sahib; But here he was to meet his match in a brave Sahib who loaded his gun calmly, and fired again and again, killing the beast.

All the Punjaubis assembled together and agreed that the Sahib was a man who appreciated and cared for others, so much so that he roamed about in the forests for our sake, in order to protect us.

Previously, many Englishmen had come here to shoot but had been disappointed,

Because the lion was very courageous and ferocious, and the Sahibs were afraid;

But for the sake of our lives, Patterson Sahib took all this trouble, risking his own life in the forest.

So they collected many hundreds of rupees, and offered it as a present to the Sahib, because he had undergone such peril, in order to save our lives.

Oh! Roshan, all the people appeared before the Sahib saying, "You are our benefactor";

But the Sahib declined to accept the present, not taking a pice of it.

So then again the Punjaubis assembled, and consulted as to how the service that the Sahib had done them could most suitably he rewarded.

And it was agreed to send all the money to England, in order that it might be converted into some suitable present,

Which should bear an engraving of the two lions, and the name of the mistari[1], head of the workmen.

The present should be such, and so suitably decorated, as to be acceptable to Patterson Sahib;

In colour it should resemble moon and sun; and that would indeed be a fit present, so that the Sahib would be pleased to accept it.

Oh! Roshan, I hope that he will accept this present for shooting the lions, as some small reward for his action.

My native home is at Chajanlat, in the thana of Domli, which is in the district of Jhelum, and I have related this story as it actually occurred.

119

Patterson Sahib has left me, and I shall miss him as long as I live, and now

Roshan must roam about in Africa, sad and regretful.

[1] Foreman-mason.

Composed by Roshan mistari, son of Kadur mistari Bakhsh, native of the village of Chajanlat, Dakhli, Post Office Domli, district of Jhelum. Dated 29th January, 1899.

Made in the USA
Lexington, KY
05 December 2012